OTAGO

DISOBEDIENT TEACHING

Surviving and creating change in education

WELBY INGS

Published by Otago University Press
Level 1, 398 Cumberland Street
Dunedin, New Zealand
university.press@otago.ac.nz
www.otago.ac.nz/press

First published 2017
Copyright © Welby Ings
The moral rights of the author have been asserted.

ISBN 978-1-927322-66-6 print

Design by Fiona Moffat
Cover and illustration by Nicole A. Phillips
Typeset by Otago University Press

Printed though Independent Publishers Group, Chicago

CONTENTS

ACKNOWLEDGEMENTS

How do you acknowledge a lifetime of learning? A book like *Disobedient Teaching* only happens because of the influence of teachers. So to those who knew that there was more to intelligence than passing level tests, I am indebted to you. I appreciated being left alone to draw pictures during sustained silent reading lessons, being allowed to stay in the bottom maths group to play with Cuisenaire rods in Form Two, and being delegated to running the nature table with unbridled freedom (except for the removal of the road-killed opossum and a floating goldfish that eventually turned from milky white to putrescent green). I am thankful for the times that I wasn't tested, for the afternoons I was allowed to do projects I was interested in, and for those instances where you showed that you cared about what I was trying to become.

These are my positive memories of early education.

I owe my mother and father a lifetime of wonder, because they refused to accept that I was stupid and they taught me to follow my imagination and to consider the impact of my actions on other people.

I am indebted to my friend Jasna Romic, who spent hours tracking down obscure references for me, correcting details and cautioning me against excess. I am also thankful to Robin Charles, Jenni Jenkins, Christine Cremen and James Wakelin for their valuable feedback on chapters in this book.

I have been inspired by Colin Gibbs, David Sinfield, Evelyn Jull, Suzanne Ings, Ron Rashbrook, Bill Packard, Desna Jury, Jim Peters, Avon Hansen, Bevan Mudie, Anne McGlashan and Brian Clarke. You are fine educators who have profoundly altered my thinking.

Unless they are mentioned above, in this book the names of teachers and students have been changed so that they are not identifiable. In organisations I have, in four instances, also changed the gender of the individual to further protect their privacy and reputation. With the exception of my youthful alma maters, Pukeatua Primary and Te Awamutu College, all other learning environments remain anonymous or have been constructed using a fictional name.

This said, it is not possible to make anonymous my greatest debt: to every student I have taught and who in turn has taught me. You may never know the impact you have on teachers. You bring humanity to ritualised curriculum, meaning to learning and the most wondrous potential to knowledge.

You are a precious thing.

Not all teachers forget you.

Example is not the *main* thing in influencing others.
It is the *only* thing.

ALBERT SCHWEITZER

PROLOGUE

a small anomaly

It is late at night. Outside you can hear the hum of commuters as they make their exodus from the city. Their tyres swish through a black skin of water still clinging to the street. I am sitting here unsure how to begin talking about productive disobedience and how it re-forms the world in which we live.

In my office the light is dim. On the walls there are small objects – eclectic scavengings, the detritus of many journeys. These are gifts I have been given because students across 40 years of teaching have known of my penchant for the unusual and neglected. They are poignant things: an old felt heart stuffed with lavender, a Julia Kristeva voodoo doll, a broken bicycle lamp brought back from the ferocity of a Soviet winter, and flowers now drained of colour, grown delicate and brittle with age. Among these objects there are two photographs, and perhaps we might begin by talking about these.

The first shows a boy. He is 10 years old. It was taken in the 1960s. In this picture he sits at a regulation wooden school desk looking up at the camera. The pencil poised in his hand is not his own, nor is the book in which he is pretending to write. Behind him, artfully arranged on the wall, are some paintings of mushrooms, but these are not his either.

The boy's father and mother were shearing contractors who worked the woolsheds of Ngaroma, Arohena, Puahue and Parawera – places most people have never heard of. At the time the photo was taken he couldn't read or write. In fact he wouldn't be able to do these things until he was 14. He was destined to live out his years in school at the bottom of the class. When he left primary school he would receive a certificate for being the bin monitor. Four years later he would be expelled from college. Although he would eventually enter teacher training, he would be suspended halfway through the programme. After his probation year of teaching he would be refused certification and he would resign. Although he would return to teaching, in subsequent years he would receive letters of admonishment from Education Boards and boards of governors. All of these were related to his propensity to break rules. There would be pickets outside one of the schools in which he taught and the protesters would demand his removal.

He would spend a lot of time fighting.

The second photo is a page torn out of *Time* magazine. It is of a man in his fifties who has just received an award. He's a professor. In the years that follow this photograph he would be given medals for his research and teaching and his PhD students would become thought leaders who changed organisations around the world.

His trajectory would be a blaze of acknowledgement. Although he would go to the same teachers' training college as the boy in the other photograph, he would graduate with distinction. Across his years in primary, intermediate and secondary teaching, educators would be ferried through his classrooms to watch the innovative approaches he took to developing learning. He would become one of the architects of the New Zealand technology curriculum, he would found an alternative school, and in 2004 he would be awarded the country's first PhD in creative practice. Today he is an advisor on creativity to a range of international business and educational organisations. The films he has created have screened at Cannes and Berlin and have been shortlisted for the Oscars. In 2001, in recognition of his contribution to education, he was awarded the inaugural New Zealand Prime Minister's Supreme Award for Teaching Excellence.

These are two very different photographs. They show two people who made life journeys through the New Zealand education system. One was a fighter and one was a negotiator, but I am not sure which of them would be better to ask about the nature of schooling in this country. Both were driven by passion. Both made unusual choices and tried to change the things that happened around them.

But if you look closely, their awkward smiles and unease in front of the camera suggest something they have in common. These are photographs of the same man. And he is professionally disobedient.

what is a disobedient teacher?

So what is this book about? Well, it's not a teaching manual or a self-help book or a treatise on New Zealand education, although you could think about it in all of these ways. Perhaps you might describe it as an arm around the shoulder of people who try to change things for the better. Perhaps somebody like you. It is concerned with the power of the disobedient teacher. Such teachers and learners are not passive or submissive, and this book tells stories about them. There are stories from the chalk face. Some are funny and some are poignant, but they all show alternative ways that teachers influence students, schools and the wider communities in which we operate. It argues for empowerment and demonstrates our ability to affect change virally.

Disobedience is a twelfth-century French word that means refusal to 'submit to a higher power or authority'. When we disobey we move beyond acquiescence. We assume that 'authority' is an insufficient argument for the abeyance of thinking and action. When we disobey we look into the heart of a situation we are encountering and we make change because we know we are empowered to do so. So I don't think disobedience is a dirty word. It is simply claiming the right to see and respond to the world in a different way. Productive disobedience is an agency that moves things forward.

Disobedient teaching is what happens when you close the door on your classroom or office and try unconventional things because your professional compass tells you that it is right. It doesn't wait for permission. It understands how systems work and it is compassionate and strong enough to take risks to make things better. It disobeys and positively changes systems. It does not tell you to remain compliant while you climb the hierarchical ladder. Disobedient teaching is rooted in the belief that you can influence things right now, from where you are. Beyond New Zealand's current obsession with micro-managing teachers and students it advocates for something better and infinitely richer. It challenges our educational preoccupation with marking, reporting and accounting. Most importantly, it shows how and why highly effective educators operate beyond these confines.

Disobedient teachers are humane, passionate, creative risk takers. They are professional in a sense of the word that reaches beyond the compliant ticking of performance indicators. They ask questions and they don't give up – and they make things better. This book looks at how and why they do it.

* * *

PART ONE

CHANGE-ABILITY

a black poppy

Let me start by telling you about the first time I was introduced to the cost of disobedience. To do so we will need to go back to a rugby field at Te Awamutu College. It was 1972. In this year James K. Baxter died, the Equal Pay Act became enshrined and Suzanne Donaldson won the Loxene Golden Disc Award. But before all of these things happened there was a lunchtime incident on the field in front of the main block that would change my life. It would be the first instalment in a progression of lessons about influencing change.

The incident occurred because my twin sister and I, having decided that attendance at the school's compulsory Anzac Day service should be optional, had organised a student peace rally. We had made 20 small, black Anzac poppies out of wire and paper, and we painted them with Indian ink stolen from the art room. Selling them to raise money for the peace movement seemed like a magnificent idea. If it was a movie it would have had a swelling 1960s soundtrack, but being rooted in the real world we were forced to make do with an anti-war poem my sister had composed and a wee jam jar containing five ten-cent coins. These were the proceeds from sales of the poppies by 12.35 in the afternoon.

My sister and I stood on the field in front of the school surrounded by a small cluster of 'cool' sixth form kids. Our chests were decorated with protest poppies and swollen with the indignation and passion that only 16-year-old adolescents can achieve. We were poised to overthrow the tyranny of the secondary school power structure.

I can still remember Mr Mitchell. He came walking across the field with one of those curious smiles that people in authority use to mask a problem. A number of the more strategic sixth formers surreptitiously unpinned their poppies, stuffed them into their pockets and dissolved into the background. When he reached us he glanced down at the opening lines of the poem:

I bought your blood red poppy and painted it death black
You child who sells the poppy, paint your soul like that.

Then he looked up. The milk of human kindness curdled on his face. With a swipe he whipped the tray of poppies aside, stamped one paper flower into the grass and marched my sister and me off to his office. The cool kids fled. Halfway across the field, when we tried to reason with him, he swung around and told us loudly that we were disrespectful and an outrage and we would be expelled.

Because my sister and I lived a long way out in the country we couldn't be sent home straightaway. The school bus didn't head off until 3.30pm. I think we spent 20 minutes being shouted at in the principal's office, then we were made to stand at the doors of the school hall, wearing our black poppies as the Anzac veterans filed in for the service. In my memory all sound has gone from this picture. It plays in slow motion. I stand looking at my sister and we are trying not to cry. Our education has come to a brutal end. The elderly people who pass between us stare with a mixture of bewilderment and disgust.

When we got home that afternoon our parents were waiting for us. The school had phoned them. We were frightened. Nothing like this had ever happened in our family. My mum and dad were good people. They worked hard so we could get an education and have opportunities they never had. We had been brought up to think about other people's feelings – and to be respectful.

Having all of the cowardice of my convictions I followed my sister as we wheeled our bicycles up the hill. I can recall the curious sound of the broken spoke clanking on my front wheel. It was like a gallows marker. When we reached the house silence descended. We looked down, and my parents looked down, and nobody moved. This was a terrible thing.

Then eventually my father spoke. He said they didn't agree with what we'd done, and my mum told us that we had hurt people and changed nothing. Then they did a curious thing. Dad took our bikes and propped them up against the side of the house. Then he turned around and told us that they were proud that we stood up for something that we believed in, even when everybody else deserted.

Then, they held us.

They taught me my first lessons about disobedience and change. If you want to alter the conditions around you, you have to learn to work with people, and you need to have people who love you.

the waiting game

Sometimes the organisations we stand up against are very strong. When we seek to change them by throwing ourselves in dramatic gestures against their values we often end up being marginalised or dismissed. This is true of teaching.

In education we often know that things are wrong. Policies and emphases are rolled out, but not all lauded ideas work. Sometimes we experience these flaws as students, sometimes as teachers and sometimes as parents. Over-assessment, systematisation, disproportionate emphasis on one way of knowing, inflexibility, limited trust, and a preoccupation with how material is presented over a focus on the humanity of learning can all operate as distortions in schools. Our anxieties hover over us when we watch our children losing hope, when we mutter in staffrooms about fashionable ideas that become unwritten policy, or when we remain silent, knowing what we are doing is flawed. We are afraid that we are not empowered to change things, or that if we disobey we will be seen as unprofessional.

But our powerlessness is an illusion. Change is possible, and ordinary people achieve it. People like you. People who think about things and imagine richer horizons. People who find themselves in cul-de-sacs and create effective ways out. People who still believe in the power of transformation.

One of the things I learned very early in teaching was that waiting for permission means very little ever gets changed. Often in organisations we are advised to tread water until we find ourselves in more secure positions. The problem, of course, is that such advice is rarely given by the kinds of people who transform the world around them.

the loyal grenadier

I remember when I was a student at teachers' college I was sent home from a practicum because I wouldn't wear a tie. In the afternoon when I caught a return bus out to the school, wearing a cravat, I found myself directed back to a disciplinary committee. I thought to myself, 'I'll wait until I get out of teachers' college, then I'm going to change some things.'

In my first year of teaching I received a reprimand from the Auckland Education Board and was told by the principal to wait until I was certificated before I tried to change anything. After I was conditionally certificated I found myself in a primary school under the watchful eye of a senior teacher, who every day walked into my classroom, tapped her wristwatch and called out 'Maths time'. I produced lesson plans that had to be left on her desk and signed before I was allowed to teach them. And with my colleagues I despondently marched my classes of small Pacific Island children around and around the asphalt to her scratchy recording of *The Loyal Grenadier*. This, she informed us, was to teach the children discipline. My friends told me, 'Wait until you get to be a senior teacher, then you can change some things.'

All this time I huddled with similarly disgruntled colleagues in groups in the staffroom. We had bought the lie that we were powerless and, as a result, we became so. We were following the paths of thousands of teachers before us, dissipating the energy that we could use to change things into criticism and complaint. Our ideas didn't take root, they didn't grow and they didn't make things better for other people. We became non-reformers who traded in our vision for a droll kind of cynicism that enabled us to survive but never altered the status quo.

We were told to wait, and we waited for something that never came.

I wonder about the rhetoric of waiting. I have friends who have become principals of schools. They have sacrificed a great deal to climb up through the ranks, yet often when we sit down together I hear them confronting the same frustrations we experienced back in teachers' college. They aren't free either. They can't move because of the Education Review Office, or parents' expectations, or boards of trustees. They end up doing things they find morally and phil-osophically questionable because they are always accountable to someone else. They are controlled by the same fear of failing that everyone in hierarchies experiences. They are afraid to disobey.

The truth is that each of us, irrespective of where we stand in an organisation, has the ability to change things. It's just a matter of studying the system around us and finding effective strategies. No teacher is powerless. It is the nature of education that we should question, and it is the nature of professionalism that we should seek to improve on practice that we recognise as flawed.

But what is it that enables certain people to change things? Well, let's have a look at this.

***

PART TWO
CREATIVITY

the disobedient thinker

Some people are disobedient thinkers. They are the shapers of our world. They create alternatives and open doors in walls that the rest of us believed were blank surfaces. They change things because they think beyond limitations. They ask questions that ordinary people don't, and they give themselves levels of permission others avoid.

Disobedient thinking is really just another way of describing creativity. It is a normal ability that we all have, and we encounter it all the time. It is a beautiful human attribute, arguably the most precious thing we possess. Being able to create is not a celestial gift granted by a divine muse who flits across the horizon and kisses the polished cheeks of a few selected artists and poets. It is an ordinary way of thinking that allows us to adapt and extend conditions that keep us constrained. Without it, evolutionarily we would never have been able to develop because we would never have moved beyond the established. This is why we feel euphoric when we encounter creative solutions. We laugh at the insightful disobedience of wit, we smile when we encounter innovative solutions to mundane problems, and we applaud creativity when we experience it surfacing through the proscribed and mediocre. We are reminded that productive disobedience broadens our world.

optimism and necessity

The ability to think disobediently is a fundamental part of being human. Historically, philosophers, inventors, economists and social reformers have questioned the limitations of what exists. They have imagined alternatives and offered solutions that have brought us to better places. Indeed, a fundamental idea underpinning the rise of liberal democracy was that greater freedom of thought would allow human beings to reach their destined levels of creative potential. This freedom to think disobediently has become a sustaining source of improvement in contemporary society. In a technologically democratised world where millions of people now have levels of agency that were never available in the past, we witness changes built on the potentials of the open-source movement. These changes, enhanced by online peer groups, now enable levels of information exchange and realisation that dissolve the levels of control that have traditionally been the prerogative of affluent elites. Such a situation advantages those who can think creatively. Disobedient thinkers who can look into the heart of what exists and conceive effective alternatives increasingly have the capacity to realise new social, economic, technological and political reforms that better meet ordinary people's needs.

the social editor

However, our natural propensity to think disobediently is constrained by something silent and controlling. It grew up with you, and it attentively stands just behind your shoulder. It is your social editor. It got in to bed with you last night and it accompanied you on your way to work this morning. It is the cautioning voice that says 'no' to your ideas because they might sound silly, or they might not work, or they might be unstable, or they might make you look like a fool. Your social editor has phenomenal power and it causes you to function at levels far below your potential. It trains you to approach problems complicitly. In the pursuit of social integration, it teaches you not to stand out and it shuts down initiatives that might potentially lead to disruption. It also suggests that you are not empowered to change things.

the perniciousness of cool

For students, this social editor often operates through the construct of 'being cool'. Being cool prescribes the way we act and think so that we fit in with sanctioned ideas. In the distorted pursuit of authentic identity, we adopt prescribed instructions about what to wear, how to look, what to value, what to think, what to buy and what to disparage. Originality is substituted by a socially endorsed replacement that has been shaped by somebody else. As kids work their way through childhood and adolescence trying to find their identity, 'cool' becomes a controlling agent and a limit on productive disobedient thinking. Taking risks that might threaten coolness is consciously avoided.

And this is why coolness is an insidious thing. While it purports to be about individual agency, coolness is actually something shaped by those who seek to align our anxieties with commercial or ideological solutions. A pernicious feature of this, of course, is that although coolness is manufactured by other people, it is policed by its victims. Vulnerable kids end up monitoring themselves and their peers, and they alienate those who don't conform.

Disobedient thinking, risk-taking and ideas that might lead to public failure are scrupulously avoided. Terms like 'loser', 'try hard', 'fail' and 'shame' become the language of peer control. And it becomes ubiquitous. The pursuit of coolness systematically discourages us from acting as significant change agents, irrespective of our age. Cool people don't take risks. They adopt, adapt and reinforce what has been pre-established, and then they pretend that it is a sign of individuality.

This policed construct of compliance has an equivalent in organisations (including schools) in the concept of the unquestioning 'team player'. While, of course, any social organisation needs people to function effectively with those around them, in dysfunctional environments team playing can come to mean substituting individual, critical action for subservience to dominant ideas and values. We are encouraged to perform obedience. When dominant ideas become threatened we are taught that thinking and operating outside the norm is unprofessional and disrespectful. If we disrupt an empowered idea, we can sometimes find ourselves framed as being undermining and unfair to our colleagues.

This phenomenon becomes particularly pronounced in damaged systems that try to preserve certain ideas as their inherent flaws become increasingly exposed. Insisting on allegiance and conformity in the name of educational professionalism is a kind of oxymoron. It is difficult to grow environments for creativity, questioning and brave individual agency when, as teachers, we feel forced to role model the opposite.

mundane disobedience

But productive disobedience is commonplace. It occurs all around us, often in mundane but very beautiful ways. Let me give you an example. The other weekend I was in town. I drive an old ute, and although it has many fine qualities, negotiating itself into parallel parks is not one of them. Well, perhaps I should take responsibility here: it's me who is no good at parallel parking. I will drive for blocks to avoid having to do it. However, on this day there was obviously some event on in the city because everywhere I searched was occupied. In the end I found myself following a woman who had come in from the country too. Like mine, her car was covered in dust but she was towing a small trailer. I instantly felt sorry for her. If my finding a park was tough, hers was going to be almost impossible.

Eventually, after driving around numerous streets of parked vehicles there appeared in front of us a small parallel space. I saw her drive forward, indicate and begin to back into the gap. Waiting some distance behind her I practised the magnanimity of a man who was about to benefit. This was because it was clear that there was no way that her car and trailer could fit into such a small space. Carefully she backed in, then got out of her vehicle and looked at the problem. Her car was still forked out on to the road. I nodded at her benevolently. Then, while I watched, she bent down, undid the draw bar, stood the trailer up on end and backed her car in. It was a perfect fit.

She had defied logic. As my smug assurance sagged behind the wheel I was concurrently struck by how creative she was. But here is an interesting thing: I suspect if I had suggested such a thing she would probably have told me that she wasn't. She may have said that she wasn't artistic, that creativity belonged to somebody else. But she had solved a problem my rational thinking couldn't.

individual genius

The disobedient nature of creative thinking has an interesting history. Up until the beginning of the nineteenth century the verb 'to create' was rarely used. It was accepted at that time that what human beings did was reason, understand, construct and, if they were lucky, detect divine patterns. But with the development of the Romantic period and its resulting emphasis on individual genius, artists began to describe themselves as 'creative'. Hence William Blake in 'Jerusalem' stated, 'I will not reason and compare, my business is to create', and William Wordsworth, in his 'Miscellaneous sonnets', said, 'creative art demands the service of a mind and heart'. These thinkers were no longer talking about adaptation. They were suggesting that something could be brought into being from nothing. Creativity came to mean a divine form of cognition, or what the British educationalist Christopher Frayling called a thinking process capable of 'challenging the gods'.

Interestingly, this claim can be paralleled to changes in the way we came to understand the concept of genius. In classical times a genius was not a person, but an independent guiding spirit. Individuals didn't attain the status of genius, but had their thinking elevated as a consequence of divine visitation.

accommodation and disruption

The identification of sophisticated, disobedient forms of thinking has, since the nineteenth century, had a rather uneasy relationship with formalised organisations (including education). Accordingly, it is not surprising that the inclusion of the word 'creativity' in curriculum documents has generally been accompanied by a distinctive blend of optimism and disquiet. Although it has been broadly accepted that creativity may be a way of defining a valued type of thinking, the nurturing of its processes and outcomes – because it is disruptive – has tended to pose difficulties. These have been most clearly pronounced when educational paradigms swing significantly towards approaches that elevate performance-based objectives and measurable processes. Because of its very nature, creativity is difficult to either orchestrate or measure.

The uneasy tension this produces in institutions, both educative and corporate, is often exacerbated by value systems that seek to maintain high levels of equilibrium. The American design theorist Ralph Caplan describes the situation like this:

> *One of the hallmarks of a creative person is the ability to tolerate ambiguity, dissonance, inconsistency and things out of place. But one of the rules of a well run corporation is that surprise is to be minimalised. Yet if this rule were to be applied to the creative process, nothing worth reading would get written, nothing worth seeing would get painted, nothing worth living with and using would ever get designed.*[1]

It is not difficult to see the paradox: any teacher required to write plans for task-oriented learning with measurable outcomes wrestles with the difficulty on a daily basis. That is why, in general, the term 'creative' tends to be dealt with in specific areas of educational documents, primarily appearing in either the broader aims and principles, or as one of a number of listed behaviours in matrices of outcomes or exemplars. Where it appears more sparingly is as a definable, exercisable and nurtured system of thinking. We say we want it, we recognise it when it arrives, but we find it very difficult to accommodate the teaching of it into an evidence-based paradigm that relentlessly infects the structure of our education system.

There are obvious reasons for this difficulty. Creative thinking is not only nebulous and difficult to massage into assessable performances. It is also often disruptive of time and resources.

trading beyond experience

The British designer Alan Fletcher has a lovely way of describing creativity. He says it is 'a compulsive human urge which demands more than ritual actions or routine responses and is only valid when one is trading beyond experience.'[2] Let's look at this for a moment. First, Fletcher recognises that creativity is natural. More importantly, he sees it as tied to a process where we 'trade beyond experience'. Here, as thinkers, we operate outside of the realms of familiarity. We function beyond expectations and assumptions, and beyond the known territory of teachers, schools, managers or organisations. We journey onto foreign landscapes, and in so doing we ask those who seek to guide us to trust in what they can't define or imagine.

When we trade beyond experience we trade with the indefinable. This can cause distinct problems for schools where systems for valuing are predicated on rewarding what can be made explicit. In evidence-based environments, creative thinkers (especially students) are forced into a difficult situation. If they stay true to the actual nature of their thinking, much of it will be immeasurable and therefore unrewardable. This is because creative thinking cannot always be made explicit (even by the thinkers themselves). This is not to say that complex thinking doesn't occur. Theorists from Michael Polanyi to Elizabeth Smith and Donald Schön have for decades shown how we think and solve problems using knowledge that we can't make explicit.

A consequence of our emphasis on assessing only what can be made tangible is that students are forced to remanufacture the process of their thinking into a narratable product. Unfortunately, what gets rewarded (and reinforced) is not *authentic* thinking at all, but the ability to construct illustrated explanations that are often quite artificial. These render invisible and inconsequential the illogical leaps our thinking makes. The flickers of unexpected inspiration, the intuitive moments of realisation and the visitations of genius count for nothing because they can't be turned into evidence. In real terms, insight is replaced by the tyranny of the narrativising workbook, the point-by-point explanation, the process-board or forced reflective journal entry that tells a documented, linear story of what was thought, what it affected and what resulted – even when this didn't happen.

Of course, the tragedy is that in pursuit of the documentable product, creative thinkers are massaged into losing touch with how they genuinely ideate and develop ideas. Instead, they are taught to become dishonest, didactic storytellers. Because creativity is often unstable and time consuming, in schools its poorer cousins are often elevated to a replacement status. We might call these forms of lower-level creativity *embellishment* and *small-scale adaptation*. Often these are not disobedient thought but a form of strategic, non-transformative thinking that institutions call creativity.

embellishment

Embellishment involves applying surface adaptation to a pre-existing idea or environment. This is generally easy for organisations to accomommodate because ornamenting ideas simply contributes to the maintainence of the established. Decoration (be it physical or conceptual) is often labelled as creative so that teachers and organisations can feel good about themselves. It is normally more controllable than creative thinking and it generally operates inside carefully prescribed variables. Thus something like a tiled wall made by students, entirely to specifications with only colour and pattern added as individual input, may be decorative and visually arresting, but it is arguable whether it encourages and grows significant levels of creative problem solving. This is not to say that such activities do not have value on social, technical or psychomotor levels, but decorating inside very formulaic restraints generates very limited levels of creative thinking. Creativity has teeth. Its instinct is to disobey established order if it senses that something better might be realised, then it moves our thinking forward by pursuing alternatives that disrupt the preimagined.

small-scale adaptation

Although embellishment is occasionally used as a substitute for creativity, small-scale adaptation is its more ubiquitous relation, and it is this that we most often practise in the name of creative learning. Small-scale adaptation simply involves amending what already exists. It places an emphasis on reviewing current solutions, being analytical and making alterations.

Normally such an approach is prefigured by teachers asking students (before they begin thinking for themselves) to study what already exists. This approach generally causes people to position their thinking dimensions inside that of others. So, before we ask a student to write a poem about spring, we might ask them to study what other poets have written about the same subject; before we prepare a body of thinking for examination we might refer people to exemplars. Similarly, before we ask children to solve a technological problem we may ask them to seek out devices that already address the situation.

This approach differs from how we develop creativity in higher levels of thinking. Let me give you an example. Imagine the interior of your home for a moment. Try to picture it in your head: where you sleep, where the morning sun first touches the house, where you store your towels. If we were to design a learning environment where you might solve the problem of making this a more pleasant space to live in, we might do one of two things.

First, I could encourage you to go out and collect images of home interiors that might be adaptable. As a first step you would look at what others have done, then probably analyse and adapt their solutions. This is a standard default position. We often trawl through magazines of other people's thinking, cut out pictures and tweak the ideas until we come up with something that seems to fit. Numerous publications on the market are dedicated to this process. They sell us other people's ideas, and we are told that these are *our* sources of inspiration. In so doing we learn (and have reinforced) a kind of creative dependency. This is small-scale adaptive thinking that leads to a kind of *re*-designing. We end up storing our towels in a different type of cupboard. This kind of problem solving can work at a certain level. It is certainly relatively safe, because fundamental problems have normally been addressed in the solutions we have gathered. But generally, when we use this approach our creativity is reduced to analysing, adapting and applying somebody else's thinking.

However, in more advanced creative thinking environments such a problem is approached very differently. The *situation* is the primary focus rather than the *solution*. For instance, we might live in our house for a year, becoming aware of the way we use the space, then we think about the things that delight us and become 'self-conscious' of our unique needs. By drawing the situation inside ourselves we wouldn't just look for a new bench top; we would think about how we work with food. We would *dwell* with the situation and it would talk to us. We would feel needs, embody problems, and experience the situation through a diversity of senses and tacit knowing.[3] From this position we would incrementally begin to create unique solutions to unique situations.

The difference in the two approaches is that small-scale adaptation operates from existing solutions to other problems, whereas creative thinking works from an origin. The outcomes are invariably very different.

growing creative thinking

So, we might ask, how on earth as a teacher do I grow such thinking? I might genuinely want to make learning rich and student-centred, and I might genuinely care about activating and exercising creative thinking, but when I think about it, most of what I teach probably falls into one of the two default descriptions already outlined.

Well, the happy truth is that it probably doesn't. It is likely that you develop productive, creative thinking opportunities all the time. It is normally a human being's predilection to default to creative thinking. In children, this permeates their play and their story telling, it emanates from them when we read or tell them unillustrated stories because they automatically co-create by imagining the world unfolding around them.

Let me show you an example. I would like to tell you a story and then I will ask you a question. You can't be wrong with your answer, but it will show you something interesting about yourself.

the troubled ruler

Many years ago, in a time now lost to record, there was a kingdom. It had been inherited by a young ruler whose father, a warrior king, had expanded the borders of his world. However, the cost of his aggression had been death and exhaustion. His people had paid a terrible price and now they wanted peace.

The young king was a considerate man, and he began designing a new, civilised city for his people that he hoped would become the flowering heart of his reign. He designed magnificent schools, free libraries, public gardens, efficient medical systems and beautiful housing. The wonders craftsmen and thinkers created were breathtaking. There were state buildings with waterfalls that wound their way through picturesque courtyards and across beautiful, cobalt-tiled, interior gardens. There were hospitals where light poured through crystal windows, fracturing into every known colour. Here every bed was a jewel of hope, and high above, in vaulted ceilings, painted birds sang in the crests of exotic trees.

But what made the young king's city so famous was its legal system. In this perfect world there was no crime. In the markets, as the evening shadows drew across the courtyards, merchants would leave their tents standing, their tables laden with produce and their wares unsecured. There were no locks on houses because people knew that in the morning everything would still be there – untouched, perfectly in place. They walked through the city on long summer nights knowing that they were safe.

Why did this happen? Well, the king had established a unique process of law. There were no criminals in this world because if a citizen was found guilty of an offence they were imprisoned deep under the city. This gaol was a great, corridored labyrinth that the King's father had built many years before. Here the miscreants lived out the remainder of their lives in dark, silent cells. They were never released.

Above ground, the city blossomed and became a jewel of civilisation. Artists, musicians, mathematicians, philosophers, botanists and architects flocked to its perfection and each contributed to its wonders. But over time the king became worried about the people he had condemned to the prison under his city. Although his systems for determining guilt seemed fair and just, he wondered if perhaps he might have trapped someone there who had been innocent. He talked to his advisors and judges but they assured him he had no need for concern. Their justice system was perfect. However, at night in dreams the question came to him, through the soft dust of sleep, pleading in silence and watching with empty eyes. He awoke each morning, haunted and worried.

Eventually, ignoring the advice of his judges, the king made his way down into the bowels of the city. He had not been in these corridors since he was a boy. They now hung with time-sagged cobwebs and their passages were rank with dust. His footsteps were absorbed by the silence. As he wound his way through tepid darkness he passed torches that flickered in stone walls, their pale flames illuminating alcoved statues of forgotten saints. He passed cells where there was no longer movement, just a few bleached bones and the scent of dying dreams. Eventually he came to the end of a large corridor where the gaoler was waiting. He was a thin man who for years had not seen the light of day. It had been his task to govern this world without question, but now the King had arrived. The man watched him approach with anxious, milky eyes. He glanced nervously at his two frail children who were huddled close beside him. They were small and thin, dressed in rags the colour of dust, their eyes strangely wide …

I am going to stop the story here. I know this is irritating, but I'd like to ask you a question. Think about this for a moment, then close your eyes if it helps you to form a better picture. In your mind's eye, look at the gaoler's two children. Look at them carefully. Look at the colour of their hair, at what they are wearing on their feet and where they are positioned in relation to their father and to each other. Now here's the question: are they two girls? Or two boys? Or a girl and a boy? Now say your answer out loud.

So, here is something interesting. In the story I never told you the answer to that question. You created it. All the way through this tale you were co-creating. The building with its interior gardens and waterfall, the market place at the end of the day, the hospital, and the corridors under the city, you created them, in subtle, nuanced detail. What you created was different to anything anybody else reading this book will ever see. You created these things because it is natural for you to do so. You create to enrich what you experience. This is a wonderful thing. You create when there are spaces for you to do so. This story was not filled with the animated pictures of cinema, prescribing sound, colour, shape and movement. Details were not locked in place by somebody else's illustrations in a picture book that pre-empted your need to imagine. The pictures you created and the information they contained were entirely yours. You created them as a normal function of thinking.

The simple point is that whenever we are caught in a cul-de-sac and can't find our way out, or whenever we seek to enrich our experience of what exists, we resort to creative thinking. As educators, managers, parents or students, when we want to develop this potential in ourselves or others we design environments without answers, and in so doing we allow the human mind to trade beyond experience.

creativity and intelligence

There is something very interesting about creative thinking and its relationship with what we traditionally measure as intelligence. Perhaps it might not come as a surprise if you have worked with highly creative individuals, but research – some of it dating back as far as the 1920s – shows us that there is *no significant correlation* between extremely creative thinkers and people who score very highly on traditional intelligence tests. Early evidence of this non-correlation surfaced in Lewis Terman's longitudinal study *Genetic Studies of Genius* (1925, 1947, 1959). Building upon the work of Alfred Binet, Terman developed the Stanford–Binet intelligence scales. His research studied 856 boys and 672 girls, who were rigorously tested to produce a research sample of what were deemed to be highly intelligent children.[4] Terman's study produced a number of interesting paradoxes, and among these was the fact that the high IQ scores of these individuals did not predict high levels of creative achievement later in life.

Subsequent studies by other researchers have reinforced Terman's conclusions, leading to what we now know as the Threshold Theory. This holds that above a certain level, intelligence does not have a significant effect on creativity. This theory is used to explain the fact that although very creative people generally exhibit comparatively high levels of intelligence, when measured by conventional intelligence tests, an IQ of 120 is generally considered sufficient for an individual to display creative genius. The non-correlation between these ways of processing thought may be due to the fact that highly creative people often think in ways that do not map easily on to conventional systems for measuring intelligence. Their propensity to process ideas divergently, to entertain multiple solutions and to resynthesise seemingly obscure connections means that their thinking does not perform well in systems that presume correct, singular answers.

Over many years while working with students, companies and organisations I have discovered some rudimentary strategies for jolting problem solving beyond adaptation or complacent first responses. I don't claim that these ideas are the sole solution to growing richer creative thinking environments, but they may be worth sharing because at a rudimentary level they are quite easy to use. They can be broadly described as disabling the obvious, making impossible marriages and conceptual challenging.

disabling the obvious

We have learned to be creatively lazy. Because few people expect us to think beyond adaptation, we often expend creative energy just far enough to reach a working solution, then we settle for that.

One easy way to deal with this problem when working with a group is to get people to disable their initial options. It is easily done. Simply ask them collectively to name the three most obvious solutions to the problem, write them up where everybody can see them, discuss them, then state that they are no longer possibilities. Normally the process of listing these ideas involves great enthusiasm, but this is followed by a slump of horror when thinkers realise that the 'easy hits' are no longer an option. This is exacerbated, of course, because they have been discussed openly, and everybody knows that everybody else has seen them. Now individuals have to genuinely start thinking in more challenging ways.

On a professional level many individual creatives do this intuitively at the outset of a problem. They note quickly what the likely response of an ordinary thinker might be, and then they remove these options from consideration. They ask questions like 'How can I look at this differently?', 'What would be unexpected?' and 'What has not been thought of yet?' In our society we call these thinkers creatives, or innovators, or entrepreneurs. Their only real concern with what already exists lies in knowing against what current thinking their unique solution must position itself. Socially and economically such people are highly valued.

impossible marriages

An impossible marriage is a technique that can be used as a way of forcing our thinking beyond the limitations of lazy connection. It involves creatively forcing a relationship between two unlikely ideas. The approach is influenced by centuries of people's observations. Consider for a moment the following insights:

A man brings together two facets of reality and by discovering a likeness between them suddenly makes them one. (Jacob Bronowski, scientist)

The history of invention can be seen as a series of marriages of incompatible ideas. (Marty Neumeier, designer)

The unlike is joined together and from the differences results the most beautiful harmony. (Heraclitus, philosopher)

You can take two substances, put them together and produce something powerfully different (table salt), sometimes even explosive (nitroglycerine). (Diane Ackerman, writer)

Creativity seems to be something which links things together ... within a new whole, which didn't exist before. (Rupert Sheldrake, biochemist)

New discoveries in science and mathematics often consist of a synthesis between theories or concepts that have hitherto been regarded as unconnected. (Anthony Storr, psychiatrist)

The more distant and distinct the relationship between the two realities that are brought together the more powerful the image. (Pierre Reverdy, poet)

... perceiving analogies and other relations between apparently incongruous ideas or forming unexpected, striking or ludicrous combinations of them. (Rem Koolhaas, architect)

... to perceive the relations between thoughts, or things, or forms of expression that may seem utterly different, and to be able to combine them ... (William Plomer, writer)

What do these observations have in common? It's an awareness of the creative potential of an impossible marriage. Here is a seemingly simple activity that illustrates the process. Look at an object in front of you. Imagine you have to create a unique advertising campaign to sell this artefact in a very memorable way. Now close your eyes for a moment and listen to what you hear around you. After 30 seconds write down one thing that you heard.

You will now have two unrelated things in front of you – two things you would normally not have brought together. Now here's the challenging part: try to use the sound to sell the object in front of you in a unique way.

You have probably just slumped. Your social editor may have just told you that this is either impossible, or silly, or too hard (or may have tried to dismiss it by making a joke of it), but put your editor aside and trust yourself for a moment. You are capable of thinking this creatively. Try constructing a simple story that combines the two things in a memorable way. You will encounter a solution quite different to the kind of idea you would normally have come up with.

Let me illustrate. Last year I was working in Melbourne with a group of young scientists. These people had been identified as potential leaders in their fields. They had been brought together on a special programme that dealt with challenging thinking. In a workshop I asked them to undertake this activity in an effort to find a new way of promoting science education. I asked them to close their eyes for 60 seconds and locate a sound. Of course I could have substituted the sound for anything they might normally not bring into consideration – something they saw on a walk, the title of a song they liked, the best present they ever received. (The point is to use something that is connected to the individual in a sensory or emotional way, because this is more likely to trigger deeper levels of tacit association.)

When they closed their eyes and listened they heard diverse things: clocks ticking, pulses beating, the sound of a truck on the street, the hum of an air conditioning system. They wrote down a sound. Then they were given five minutes of complete silence to put together a story that could be told as a YouTube commercial that would promote science to young kids in a memorable way.

Initially there was an obligatory pause as their editors kicked in, but they soon began sketching or writing. I told them that they couldn't be wrong. The aim was to be unique and arresting. They knew at the end of five minutes they would need to pitch their idea to the person next to them.

It is easy to tell euphoric stories about such activities, but there were, in truth, 20 young scientists in that room and 20 amazing pitches. I remember one in particular. When her eyes were closed a young microbiologist had noted the sound of an air conditioner. This is how she sold science education to secondary school students:

A girl is sitting in a sterile room working under the hum of a ventilator. She is supposed to be doing her homework. Bored, she distractedly runs a wet eraser around the lip of a glass of water. It sings. Using a pivot she distractedly constructs a device where her pencil taps in rhythm against a teaspoon … then as a melody of mechanical sounds grows, she rapidly arranges more and more objects that operate as levers, cams and pulleys until her room becomes an increasingly vibrant symphony of sound. As the music builds, so does her ingenuity. Eventually, pulsing as a contemporary music video, the advertisement ends with a tag line saying, 'Science – The Rhythm of Your Life'.

This from a microbiologist.

This may sound very sophisticated, so perhaps we might pull the concept of an impossible marriage back to something more fundamental. I have found that you can sit with a seven-year-old child and play a simple game that exercises this skill. Take any object they can see – anything. Ask them to name two other objects in the room and make up a story that combines all three. Often they will respond to this more quickly than adults. They can create stories very quickly about a broken doll, a cat's dish and an old sock. Every time they make an unusual connection in their story, comment on how unexpected or clever it was. Reinforce the cleverness of their ability to connect things in unusual ways. They will gather momentum very quickly. I have had whole classes of seven-year-olds hanging out for the start of a morning game where people stand up, receive three nominated objects and launch into a three-minute story. It just takes practice. Impossible marriages are very adaptable.

conceptual challenging

Conceptual challenging is basically about asking the kinds of questions we tend to avoid. As we become better able to think creatively, these challenges can become quite complex. In a design agency in which I worked in the 1990s we were asked one morning to create a piece of garden furniture based on the *melody* of the *scent* of a rose. Conceptually this was very challenging. Most of us could connect the smell of a rose to the design of a chair, but not something as abstract as the melody of a scent. I think everybody's response was to try and cut one of the difficult variables out. Creatively it felt too tough. But such challenges are commonly used when exercising high-end creative thinking because they force us to deal with very abstract syntheses.

We know historically that many ideas have been born from abstract or seemingly disassociated thinking. Nikola Tesla identified the concept of the rotating magnetic field while quoting poetry to a friend. John Gowan described the experience like this:

> *As he was walking toward the sunset quoting these words, the idea came like a flash of lightning and the solution to the problem of alternating current motors appeared before him as a revelation. He stood as a man in a trance, trying to explain his vision to his friend … The images that appeared before Tesla seemed as sharp and clear and as solid as metal or stone. The principle of the rotating magnetic field was clear to him. In that moment a world revolution in electrical science was born.*[5]

Both Albert Einstein and Max Ernst also appear to have relied on this kind of creative abstraction. Einstein discovered the theory of relativity by picturing himself riding on a ray of light, and Ernst's developments in the 1920s were heavily influenced by the consideration of random rubbings of the texture of the wooden floorboards in his room.

In higher-level creative thinking we often exercise our ability to connect abstract ideas in productive ways. Here, we are not connecting the physically experienced but working entirely with imagined concepts. At a very basic level, an activity I sometimes use with business people when exercising this skill is to ask them to package an idea. It's very simple. They have 24 hours to think of any idea, but it must be kept absolutely secret. Then they have to find a way of packaging it so whoever opens it will clearly understand what is inside. They cannot cut corners by using the written word. The packaging has to do all of the talking.

If this sounds tough, it is. But we have the ability to solve problems like this. In this instance people secretly packaged courage, or being blind, or falling in love. The next day they asked someone to silently open their package in front of the group. Nobody was allowed to say anything. People in the room simply wrote down on a piece of paper the idea they believe had been communicated and gave it to the problem solver. By reading these, the creator could evaluate the clarity of his or her communication.

I have seen many powerful solutions to this challenge, often from quite unexpected people. There was a box made of panel steel that tore tissues as you pulled them out. It packaged 'inconsolable grief'. There was a small cargo case that you unpacked, and suddenly you were unexpectedly photographed by a hidden camera flash – for 'capture'. There was a lethal-looking rat-trap apparently loaded with a small wrapped present secured to the trigger – for 'trepidation'.

Wonderful things, by wonderful thinkers.

At the outset, such problem solving can sound difficult because in formal educational environments we don't systematically exercise creative thinking. But such abilities can be nurtured and developed. The initial pedagogical challenge is to give people permission to disobey both conventional thinking and the protestations of their social editor. The results of projects like this are generally surprising because they highlight unique kinds of thinkers who often don't profile prominently in conventional contexts.

Growing such thinking is important because creativity is not the result of a mythological cultural gift, tied up with a piece of number eight wire and a bit of austerity. It is a skill, not a national attribute. If we want creativity, we have to do more than aspire to it or identify it when it arrives. As educators we have to come to terms with its nature and strategically grow it. It demands that we question and take risks and trade beyond experience. Perhaps more than this, it requires courage, unrelenting courage, a belief in possibility, and a preparedness to fail and to work with the failure of others. All of this in schools that often fear deeper levels of disruption. To achieve such a change relies on the transformative power of productive disobedience.

* * *

PART THREE
ASSESSMENT

I f we consider creativity as a form of productive disobedience, we are presented with questions about the world in which we might grow it. Traditional education has shied away from the instability necessary to develop deep creative thinking. Accordingly, where we encounter fertile environments for growing creativity in schools, they are generally the result of the persistence, ingenuity and strength of individuals (or sometimes small clusters of teachers). However, these people are forced to operate in a largely antithetical environment, heavily shaped by values based upon explicitness, data-driven assessment and accountability. Given this situation, perhaps it is useful to take a look at what we have come to call assessment.

Let's start with something historical.

lions, cheetahs and rhinoceroses

At Pukeatua Primary, where I went to school, the incinerator was over by the fence. It was an old iron contraption with a chimney, and a little door that opened for feeding in the rubbish. It was replicated in a hundred schools in a hundred districts all around this country. Back in 1962, at Pukeatua Primary there were also lions, cheetahs and rhinoceroses. They lived in Room 3 and sat at desks in lace-up shoes. The lions and cheetahs, who made up most of the class, didn't have much to do with the incinerator, but Nigel Terpstra and I, who were rhinoceroses, did. As the only members of the bottom group we were delegated the dubious responsibility of being rubbish monitors. We learned how to cook our apples on the hot plate, how to smoke the teachers' cigarette butts and, in times of crisis, when Nigel Terpstra got an asthma attack from inhaling too much cigarette smoke, we learned that holding him under the macrocarpas to breathe in the excess oxygen didn't work.

We were a result of the sixties, a decade in New Zealand schools that saw a clear push towards reassessing the highly streamed nature of education. J.C. Daniel's essays on the effects of streaming in the primary school were widely cited in the argument for continued social promotion and mixed-ability grouping.[6] Unfortunately, at Pukeatua Primary and in many other schools up and down the country, what happened was that groups one, two and three were simply replaced by lions, cheetahs and rhinoceroses (or their equivalent), and eventually most of the rhinoceroses woke up to the fact that a fancy name still equated with being at the bottom of the pile.

Being at the bottom of the pile isn't much fun. It's the place where many of us have found ourselves at some time in our schooling, and it's the place where we are most unmotivated to learn. Nearly all of us have come through school systems that use comparative methods of assessment, and most of us have learned that they do one thing very well: they teach us that we are not as good as other people. They teach us that in the race for learning, there are winners and losers and, as in most races, the losers outweigh the winners. To illustrate this, one has only to stop for a moment and think: What did I learn at school that I was no good at? Was it mathematics, or English, or chemistry? And if it wasn't, did a belief in my incompetence come from one of those competitive, peripheral obligations, the cross-country race or the school speech contest? These were the annual institutions that sent generation after generation staggering from the stage or the playing field, lowly ranked and firmly convinced that they were innately incompetent. Every year the few were lauded and the majority defeated.

But, you know, if we could go back to Room One, on any weekday morning, we would probably see ourselves in front of the class, giving morning talks or running frantically around the playground. It would never have entered our heads that by the other end of this education conveyor belt we would have come to believe that we were failures. Back then we were all orators and endurance runners, all cheetahs in the wind, and nowhere was there a rhinoceros on the horizon.

the mark factory

So why do we create rhinoceroses? Well, there is a lot of pressure in teaching to mark people and divide them into categories. It comes from schools with their need to meet Ministry of Education requirements, from parents who believe that learning is competitive, and from kids who have become convinced that a B+ or a Merit means that they are better mathematicians or writers than their peers.

Every year we fill up registers with class lists and test results. We set exams and design teaching plans around generating these marks, and in the end we hand them over to students and ourselves as an indication of their competence. By the same token (despite the rhetoric of politicians), these numbers are often used by parents as a method of assessing a teacher's ability and a school's potential.

The institution of marking is so ingrained in education that most New Zealanders believe that these grades are indications of their true ability. Despite the decades of educational studies and working alternatives, we still continue to place an inordinate amount of emphasis on comparative marking (either comparing students to other students or to pre-established criteria). We change by changing the language. Scaled percentages are replaced by raw marks, that are replaced by grades, that are replaced by levels of merit … but the fundamental premise remains the same: we preoccupy ourselves with measuring the performance of learning. We assume that what is demonstrated is what is known. As a consequence we elevate what can be made explicit and what can be narrated, and somewhere in there we miss the point that learning is not a performance. It is a process.

So how did we end up in this situation?

judgement day

If we were to travel back to a classroom somewhere between 1877 and 1904 we might witness the interesting precursor to all of this. It was known colloquially as the 'Day of Judgement'. At primary schools up and down the country Education Board inspectors arrived with papers and schedules. Annually they examined every child. Those who passed were moved up to the next class; those who failed were forced to repeat the year. Because the results of these tests were often published in local newspapers there was high pressure on children to pass, and those who did not were publicly humiliated. In schools, anxious teachers scrubbed floors, decorated classrooms with fresh flowers and strategically displayed examples of the best art and writing. Desks were cleaned and parents dressed their children in their best clothes.

This process of being marked by an outside authority took deep root in our educational consciousness. By 1899 the government had introduced the Proficiency and Competency exams into primary schools. Up until 1936 the marks from these tests determined whether a child got the opportunity to access further education. During this period New Zealand also introduced Junior Civil Service examinations (1905–12) and Public Service Entrance or Intermediate examinations (1913–36). These gave those students who had made it through to secondary school access to increasingly advanced education. Success was determined by a mark.

Then in 1944 Matriculation arrived (this was later replaced by University Entrance). These examinations operated as gatekeepers for access to university. Hard on the heels of Matriculation, in 1946, the preoccupation with marking became even more deeply embedded with the arrival of School Certificate. For many New Zealanders who traditionally left school at 15, the marks from these tests became their final experience of education. The written exams launched them with indicators of competence or failure based on a percentage. Their personal and professional identities became prescribed by whether these marks were over or under 50.[7] They learned that they were not good at chemistry or were average at English or good at geography. Marking and belief in its veracity became a socially embedded 'truth'.

Then in 2002 the National Certificate of Educational Achievement (NCEA) arrived, with its emphasis on internal assessment and measuring skills not taken into account in existing systems. But despite the vision of educational design at the turn of the century,[8] in many secondary schools (and in large numbers of tertiary institutions) students continued to sit in rooms having their performances measured based on three-hour responses to pre-set questions.

before the mark

But here is an interesting thing. Marking does not have a long historical inheritance. In fact, the academic historian George Pierson notes that the first grades (*optimi, second optimi, inferiores* and *pejores*), issued at Yale, were only given out in 1785. The assigning of actual marks to students' work appears to have been developed three years later, by William Farish at the University of Cambridge.[9]

So if assigning marks hasn't always been associated with learning, how were students traditionally assessed? Well, they were assessed in a manner close to how educators really do it today. Teachers talked to students, and they watched, listened and made informed, subjective estimations. Assessment was associated with demonstration, discussion and reflexive learning.

In medieval times, in universities like Oxford and Cambridge, all examinations were oral and public. Following a process of challenge and defence, students were expected to argue their thesis. They weren't marked. The verbal interrogation and jousting went on for up to two hours, and adjudication occurred at the same event.[10] Today this system is partially preserved in many PhD examinations, where there are no marks, percentages or grade-point averages. A candidate presents and defends their thesis to a company of scholars, who deliberate on the thinking and either award the degree or not. They read what has been written and question the candidate in depth to ascertain the veracity and integrity of their thinking. Sadly, only at this highest level of education is there still this appreciation of the need to operate beyond the realm of marks. In a PhD, learning is assessed as an integrated whole.

the influence of value

Reporting using marks actually tells us very little. We learn nothing about the nature of an individual's learning, nothing about 'how' they think and little about their approaches to problem solving. Marks become a substitute for insightful description. They replace educational analysis with comparability, providing us with data that we can rank, equate and contrast.

Where the inherent value of learning becomes negligible, marks become a substitute motivation. Despite being an abstraction they are experienced as concrete, because in the end they are what is rewarded. Students work for them. They want to know what content will be in a test. If what they study is directly related to the marking, they will understand its value and concentrate on it. They make assessments about what will be 'worth' learning based not on its intrinsic value but on its capacity to earn them marks. Accordingly, they end up demonstrating selected pieces of learning and being rewarded for a dumbing down of their educational potential. In this system, the value of what is learned doesn't really matter any more because reward is not related to what is intrinsic, only to what is performed.

Unfortunately, 'getting good marks' has become a major pre-occupation of politicians, of low-level educational reformers and, tragically, of students themselves. But if we think deeply we are left with a nagging question: with this emphasis on performing and testing, what is sacrificed? What at the heart of education pays the price for this tradition of comparison?

Well, it is learning. It is learning with its multi-layered, idiosyncratic relationships, with its messy edges and complex trajectories. It is learning that is not standardised, never experienced the same way by two individuals, never timed the same way, and is always most insightfully understood in the context of the learner. It is learning as a process, *not* a product.

standard rule

The overuse and misuse of standardised comparative testing has many critics.[11] In New Zealand, especially since the 1990s, much has been done to moderate its use (in contrast to countries such as the US, England and Wales).[12] However, it still wields significant influence. Beyond its capacity to be mishandled in decisions of accountability and effectiveness, including ill-considered proposals by politicians that teacher quality in New Zealand should be measured by marks produced in testing,[13] it can also lead to a narrowing of the curriculum and the breadth of thinking we provide for learners. This is because teachers, in an effort to be seen as effective, find themselves caught in ethical and professional dilemmas. They encounter explicit or tacit instructions and incentives to 'teach to the test' because that is what will be rewarded. Despite assertions that standardised testing can be used without it distorting curriculum and teaching, the truth is that often what is not tested is not taught. Moreover, training in the rituals and devices of testing becomes a silent but valued part of the curriculum.

Internationally such narrowness is not a given. If one considers the 25 years of educational reform initiatives in Finland, we see a country that has produced an education system that achieves among the highest rankings for equality and excellence in the world.[14] In this system there is no tracking of students during their common basic education. Children are not measured at all for the first six years, and the only mandatory standardised test is taken when they are 16. Classes are not streamed, and the difference between the weakest and strongest students is one of the smallest in the world.[15]

Significantly, there is no merit pay for teachers' performance. Finnish educators are not monitored or rated according to test results, and although they follow a basic national curriculum, they have a great deal of autonomy over how they develop methods for learning and evaluation.

constraint and divergence

If freedom from high levels of testing and reporting can have such a significant impact on an education system like Finland's, we might be left asking why we continue to hold so rigidly to a belief in the merits of standardised examination in this country. We know that it narrows what is valued and taught, and we know that it has a profound impact on higher-order learning. William Ayers notes that such tests:

> *can't measure initiative, creativity, imagination, conceptual think-ing, curiosity, effort, irony, judgment, commitment, nuance, good will, ethical reflection, or a host of other valuable dispositions and attributes. What they can measure and count are isolated skills, specific facts and function, content knowledge, the least interesting and least significant aspects of learning.*[16]

The difficulty is that standardisation assumes a high level of convergence. The divergent, deep-questioning and intellectu-ally disobedient thinker either performs within the realm of the expected or pays a substantial price. The student is forced to trade inside the limitations of what has been pre-imagined and predetermined. Many gifted children pressured by the overuse of such testing get bored and angry. Some become cynical; some disheartened. More perniciously, some begin to conceive of themselves as flawed. A system predicated on predefined criteria, levels and exemplars lacks the flexibility for genius. The very innovation and excellence it purports to value, it also constrains and punishes. This limiting of disobedient thinking is toxic to any system that seeks to grow highly intelligent, creative beings.

the illusion of success

However, standardised tests and the rankings they provide can make people feel very secure. When we do well (either as an individual, school or nation), we feel valued – and New Zealand does quite well internationally. We like marks when they suggest that we are better than other people. So long as we don't ask awkward questions about whether these marks adequately describe learning, the rankings they generate are easy to understand, easy to report, and therefore easy to use politically.

However, it is useful to think about what standardised test results actually do, especially when they operate on a global basis. A useful case in point is the OECD's Programme for International Student Assessment (PISA) and the rankings that result from it. PISA is the world's largest standardised assessment system. It has been jointly developed by participating countries and it was first implemented in 2000. It compares the test results in reading, mathematics and science of 15-year-olds in nations and regional education systems around the world.[17] Every three years the results are anxiously awaited and closely scrutinised.

While politicians often cite these results and education systems are adjusted in the light of them, standardised testing systems such as PISA are deeply criticised by many leading educationalists. In 2014, in an open letter to Dr Andreas Schleicher (the director of the programme), 83 educational academics outlined their concerns about the impact of the tests and called unanimously for a halt to the next round of examination.[18] These critics included many of the brightest and most respected educational researchers in the world. They noted that since its establishment in 2000, PISA had contributed to an 'escalation in such testing and a dramatically increased reliance on quantitative measures.'[19] In addition, they argued that its three-year assessment cycle had significantly 'distorted education policy in many countries and caused a shift of attention to short-term fixes designed to help a country quickly climb the rankings, despite research showing that enduring changes in education practice take decades to come to fruition'.[20] But, perhaps most markedly, the critique noted that by emphasising a narrow range of measurable aspects of education, standardised testing such as PISA 'takes attention away from the less measurable or immeasurable educational objectives like physical, moral, civic and artistic development, thereby dangerously narrowing our collective imagination regarding what education is and ought to be about'.

But in New Zealand many people still wait anxiously for these rankings. They are reported extensively in our newspapers, and on radio and television. Politicians are quick to use them to justify policy or attribute blame for failure. Given all the attention, we are encouraged to believe that these results mean something.

But do they?

Well, only if you narrow what constitutes a valid assessment of education down to what happens as a result of two-hour written tests of 15-year-old children. To do this you have to buy into the idea that it is acceptable that the data for these results comes from students sitting in massed examination rooms, demonstrating learning in limited timeframes, linked to nominated questions. Issues like examination stress, differences in time required for different learners' levels of reflection, and variations in the amount of pre-training for examinations have to be brushed under the carpet. Concerns related to the reliability of language translation given students' differing interpretations of the same information also have to be put aside. As do concerns over the fairness and logic of assessing very different countries, cultures and economies alongside one another, or, by extension, producing a single composite grade to represent nations that do not have uniform educational quality across all socio-economic groups. These issues often end up in the 'you're being awkward' basket. But they are real concerns, because they distort data.

But knowing this, let's just pretend for a moment that there is nothing wrong. Let's imagine that international standardised tests are valid and reliable, and that they tell us what we need to know about the quality of our education system. If this is the case, then considering our pursuit of a highly evidence-based, testing-oriented approach in New Zealand, these marks should show just how far we have progressed. So let's have a look at this.

In 2000, when the PISA survey was first instituted, New Zealand ranked third in the world in reading literacy (just behind Finland and Canada); in mathematical literacy we were also third and in science literacy we were sixth.[21] This sounded pretty good. We patted ourselves on the back. Despite being a small country, our education system outstripped the US, UK and Germany. We were standing on top of the world.

So after 16 years of a preoccupation with assessing evidence we should now be in extraordinary shape. If higher standards are the 'right' goal, and the strategy employed to achieve these has been a regime of heavy testing in the pursuit of a rise to the very top of international league tables, what does the evidence tell us? An accountability-driven environment must surely take account of these things. We must have done well. Haven't we?

Well, no, we haven't. We have rolled *down* the PISA rankings. But perhaps before we wring our hands, we should remember how flawed these tests are. We need to consider what is actually tested and how. Just as importantly, we should be aware that across a decade and a half, many countries have implemented policies clearly designed to advantage their students in these tests. However, putting these complications aside for a moment, let's have a look at the statistics.[22] Compared to our third place in the international ranking for reading literacy 17 years ago, we are currently sitting at number 10.[23] However, things are much worse in mathematical literacy. New Zealand has dropped from third down to 21st position. Finally, from our placing of sixth in the world in science literacy in 2000, we have dropped to 12th position, behind countries like Estonia, Vietnam and South Korea.[24]

So in an evidence-based system the evidence suggests that something is wrong. But when these results were released, did we wring our hands and begin to ask if the obsessive emphasis on testing in our schools was doing damage to our international rankings? No. We didn't. Or did we ask ourselves what standardised systems for measuring learning actually examine? No. We didn't do that either. What we did was blame each other. The reigning National party blamed the Labour party for the damage resulting from its long-term initiatives, and the Labour party in turn blamed National for the failure of their short-term solutions.[25]

I suggest that these results actually tell us very little. I am only discussing them here as an example of the kind of distortion that has been allowed to reinforce a flawed approach to education in New Zealand.

Understanding and evaluating learning is, of course, much more complex than what can be reported in a series of two-hour tests, irrespective of how many facilities are introduced to address corruption and deal with its variables. We should not be using such devices to understand and evaluate learning, teaching and government policy. Education is too complex for such simplistic yardsticks. No education system should be assessing itself using data gathered by sitting a child at a desk for two hours and pretending that what they write summarises their learning. The idea is ridiculous.

measurement and dependency

Of course an obsession with marks produces another, arguably deeper, problem. Because we place such high emphasis on rewarding outcomes over the *process* of thinking, most of us leave the school system ill prepared to be life-long learners (despite aspirational rhetoric to the contrary). Instead, we are trained in the formulas and rituals of testing. We learn what is being asked for and what we need to do to display the required ability. Through an insistent emphasis on performing for marks we become dependent. Deeply dependent. We wait anxiously to hear how good we are because our sense of educational achievement has become reliant on outside verification.

This is a problem, because despite the fact that the average New Zealander spends 12.6 years in school,[26] at the end of that time they actually know very little about themselves as learners. *Very little.* Think about this for a moment. It is a frightening thing. Ask yourself how much you actually know about the *way* you learn:

- Do you know what causes you to retain certain information?
- Do you know how you increase chances for discovery in what you do?
- Do you know your most effective strategies for learning from failure?
- Do you know how you push yourself beyond competence?

Are these questions difficult to answer? Probably. If you *can* answer some of them, ask yourself: 'Did somebody consciously help me gain insight into this at school?' Probably not.

These questions probably feel like very unfamiliar territory. After all of your years inside the intimate experience of your own learning, in a system that assures you of your 'learner centredness', these questions are tough for you to answer. You probably don't know the answers. What you probably *do* know, however, is how well you did when marking came around.

So herein lies a problem. If we don't know *how* we learn, then we remain reliant on somebody else to direct us. We depend on verification. We need direction and approval. Our intellect and its growth – arguably the greatest gifts we possess – are sold out to somebody else's value system, and we are systematically massaged into compliance.

the massaged mark

In considering the implications of an education system that has become overly focused on assessing performance we are faced with one other problem. This is the awkward issue of corruption. While most educators prefer to pretend that massaging marking doesn't happen, in truth it does, and behaviour associated with it is widespread.[27] Some of us have experienced it as students, and some of us encounter it in the schools in which we work.

The reason such corruption occurs is perhaps best explained by Campbell's Law. Donald Campbell was an American social psychologist, methodologist and philosopher who in 1975 developed a law that noted: 'the more any quantitative social indicator is used for social decision-making, the more subject it will be to corruption pressures and the more apt it will be to distort and corrupt the social processes it is intended to monitor'. Put very simply, if you set up fixed measurements for a social agent such as education, people within the system will begin to corrupt it so that it works in their favour.

Public schooling in New Zealand was developed as a hierarchical structure. Salaries and privilege were locked into the design of this system, and value was measured by what could be made explicit. Within this structure people learned to compete for attention and promotion. As schools morphed across subsequent decades, teachers were formally and informally assessed on the quality of student grades. Good teachers, it was assumed, taught students who performed well in tests. Because professionalism was associated with the attainment of good grades, when things became difficult, teachers and schools learned to 'work' the system.

At its most transparent, this involved the deliberate training of students in examination strategy and the prioritising of material that teachers knew would be tested. These became explicit undertakings that troubled few people, even though we know that such initiatives skew the reliability of results against students who are not similarly engineered. These behaviours continue to be instituted as a way of distorting results inside standardised systems of measurement and reward. They become deeply embedded and eventually assimilated into the practice of education. As a consequence, teachers often feel obliged to adopt such practices because they care about the opportunities high performance will provide for students in their care. They also care about their own professional profiles. However, there are arguably more damaging instances of exclusion and marginalisation that teachers and schools use more covertly to advantage their performances.

Mr Shiffol's laurels

I would like to give you an example. Before I do, though, I would like to make it clear that I worked with Mr Shiffol and he was an honourable man. In the small town where I taught in the 1980s he was valued as a caring and responsible person. He volunteered for community projects and acted as a justice of the peace. He was the head of a department in which some of my colleagues worked. He was proud of his position. Every year his students gained the top grades in his subject in the school and ranked well above the national average. On a graph of performance his results were constantly tapping against the top line.

Mr Shiffol seemed to have found a magic formula – and perhaps he had. Because of his position he set the timetable and annually populated his classes with 'high-performing' students selected from the preceding year (with one or two exceptions prominently distributed across the classes of other teachers in his department). Where he ended up with an unexpected or token underachiever he talked them into the benevolent option of a non-examined, alternative pathway. This was always presented as a caring and pedagogically compassionate gesture, because he wanted them to get the most out of their education and he was worried about the stress that examination might place on them. In the rare case where a student or parents resisted his offer, he explained that their child's performance was too low to qualify for sitting the end-of-year examination. If that didn't work, he eventually moved them to another class so they were not made to feel polarised by the high performance of their peers operating in his class. In one worst-case scenario, when even these strategies failed, he simply wore a defiant student down with expressions of exasperation and subtle ridicule. The girl packed up and left by mid-year.

Mr Shiffol hated to see people fail.

The interesting thing was that, in the community, parents thought Mr Shiffol was an excellent teacher, the school hierarchy admired him, and so did the students (even those he massaged away from his classroom). The marks were evidence of a great educator, and students scrambled to be selected for his class.

In an ethically conflicted way many of his colleagues also admired him, because his techniques for survival and distortion were so convincingly masked. He was very generous with advice. He gave workshops to other schools on 'professional development' and he was invited to be a member of numerous curriculum working committees. Mr Shiffol modelled strategic self-promotion, and edited stories of classroom experience and current educational vision. But he wasn't a bad man. He had simply learned to survive in a system that wasn't prepared to look deeply into what constituted quality learning. In a position of power he was able to make important decisions that preserved his potential for high performance.

This may be why no one understood when one year, on the morning after Guy Fawkes celebrations, he awoke to find on his lawn a half-burned effigy. It had been retrieved from a fire the night before. The polyester jacket was charred and twisted into a melted memory of itself. In the painted mouth, in recognition of his fondness for cigars, there was an unlighted firecracker. But the most distressing detail was that somebody had scrawled in angry crayon on a sign around his neck, 'Shiffol-Shithole'.

Fifteen years later I returned to the high school for a reunion, still remembering the incident. It was great to see everybody again. Many students I had known had done wonderful things with their lives, but what struck me was the significant shift in their thinking. Almost without exception they referred to Mr Shiffol in disparaging terms. The scrawled name on the card around the effigy's neck had become his moniker. The respect of these young men and women now focused on other teachers: those who had spent time with them, who had supported them through failure and who cared about them as people. Across the inevitable shakedown that time provides, Mr Shiffol's pedestal had collapsed.

stories from the whiteboard

The underperformers that Mr Shiffol weeded out each year come in many guises, but the education system ensures they are identifiable with updated marks that designate their value. These students are the product of an under-critiqued regime of marking and they constitute a kind of educational 'fall-out'. The phenomenon has been much documented and is often associated with stories of damage to students who early in the system are relegated to the bottom of the pile. But the destruction is more pervasive and subtle than this, and I would like to illustrate it by telling you two stories. They are still fresh in my mind because I encountered them last year, but when I thought about them I realised that we see students like these (albeit in different guises) many times, at many levels in the education system. You will probably recognise them.

Alice

Alice was a success. She knew it. As a child she joked that everything she produced was stuck on the fridge door with a magnet and each thing reminded her of her unwavering specialness. By five she had learned that 'even shit got put up there if you pretended it was good'.

Through primary school Alice danced a flamboyant waltz with literacy and numeracy. She learned early to read agendas and to discern formulas. Her diet of reward became a gluttony for accolades. Her education was designed for success. Teachers did everything they could to ensure it, and she learned very quickly. She entered into contracts to perform what was asked, to check the criteria, to understand the values and to deliver the goods. She found it all increasingly boring, but she got what she needed.

Alice was one of the most anxious people I have ever worked with. In our first meeting she reminded me that she had the highest grade point average of anybody entering the postgraduate programme and she was insistent that she would expect to vet any examiners selected to assess her work. If a supervisor challenged her, she asked for them to be removed because they 'didn't get' the complexity of what she was doing. But in fact Alice played things safe. This is because she had been strategically trained to be risk free. To mask her anxiety, she treated with contempt anything that threatened her chances of the perfect performance, including thinking that might take her into unstable territory.

She was very clear. She wanted a postgraduate degree and she wanted an A+. She wanted to know upfront what she needed to do for this and she designed a thesis that (on the surface) would operate as a showcase and ensure the required outcome. Things began to come unstuck for her when, early in the year, people began to ask insightful questions about her research. Initially she used contempt to dismiss them, but when that didn't work she began to absent herself from group critiques because she said that they wasted her time.

The problem lay in a simple and horrible fact. Alice had become a victim of excellence. Her life in education had become a prescribed experience of success and now she found herself with a thesis that required her to take risks. Serious risks. She needed to trade beyond experience, and as part of this she needed to fail and critically reflect on what had happened. But Alice didn't know how to fail, and, accordingly, she could neither analyse failure nor manage critical recovery. She also had little insight into how she learned. An education based on comparison and 'excellence' had denied her these things.

When her thesis was externally examined, none of the examiners gave her the A+ she felt she deserved. She blamed them, she blamed her supervisors, she blamed the institution, she blamed her peers and she blamed the literature. She lodged appeals and she threatened legal action. She wasn't interested in the examiners' three-page reports that discussed her thinking. She didn't get the mark she needed.

The fallout from unrelenting success is hard to manage as an educator. Anxiety can often hide behind an articulate façade. Having excelled in the system, students like Alice know (on very sophisticated levels) how to avoid facing what they can't control. They continue to frantically tick the boxes when the room begins to collapse, and it can be hard to reach them. Because they think they know how the 'system' works they can be contemptuous of it. Often they also have diminished levels of trust.

Here was a gifted young woman crippled by a history of protection. Unfaltering 'excellence' had become a kind of nemesis that prevented her from learning beyond a certain point. She graduated from the degree heartbroken and angry. She had been betrayed.

There was no A+ on the mark sheet. She was the cherished product of formula and contract, and it no longer worked. It wasn't fair.

Kane

Kane's case shows the other side of the coin. I met him in the autumn of 2016. His parents had come to see me. He was 17 and in trouble with the police. Although I currently work at a university, every year I try to mentor at least one student who has been expelled from secondary school or has fallen through the cracks. It's not being noble. It happened to me and I try to do something personal about it.

Kane's hands were recently tattooed, he had a couple of teeth missing and he spoke with the purity of a septic tank. He was also a gifted artist. He wanted to get into design school, but his exit from secondary school had ended earlier that year with a row of smashed windows in the English block and something unpleasant left on the back seat of the principal's Toyota Corolla.

Kane was funny. When he talked he could pull pictures out of the air. He painted wonders with words. But he had spent his life in remedial classes. He couldn't read or write. Well, that is what his reports said. But when I listened to him, his use of language was extraordinary and his design thinking was very sophisticated.

One afternoon he surprised me after I had given him a book on the work of the artist Mark Ryden to look at. He spent a couple of hours in my office sprawled on the sofa, devouring it, and when we came to talk about it he was animated. But I gradually realised that the questions he asked came from the written text. He had *read* the thing – the whole book.

I didn't understand, and then he told me something. When he was at primary school he had trouble reading and writing. Because he was measured by 'literacy' he found himself labelled as 'challenged'. He was tested constantly. At the end of each year a progression of teachers ritually lifted his final mark a little to show that he had improved under their tutelage, and next February it would plummet again. Because Kane watched other children trying hard and looking like fools when they failed, he learned to protect himself. He approached the unrelenting experience of testing and marking with a grunt and a shrug of his shoulders. He learnt to say, 'I don't know.' He told his teachers he was stupid. He performed stupidity. He was recorded as stupid. Stupidity became a protection against shame. He was very good at it. He could joke about it at school and in that process he could retrieve some degree of dignity.

When he got to secondary school the ritual continued, but because the frequency of testing was suddenly reduced he began reading on the quiet, mainly graphic novels, comic books and technique-based art books. He still thought he couldn't read and he still performed stupidity whenever assessment events arrived. The marks meant nothing to him. There is little intrinsic value in a D or a fail or a 'not achieved'. Through Years 9, 10 and 11 he became angrier and angrier. He flicked tests aside like irritations, put up with what he had to, and mocked as much as he could, including his own potential to learn.

productive disobedience

These stories and hundreds like them are not anomalies. We all know them. The damage done by obsessive testing affects many students. But it is very easy to sit back and criticise. Of course testing has a place (especially when it is used as a diagnostic tool), but great teaching is concerned with effectiveness, and its primary emphasis is on informal watching, questioning and assessing *inside* the practice of learning. Teachers know that learning is nuanced, cumulative and highly integrated. They know that its complexity cannot be reliably assessed against standards, indicators of progression, or the provision of nationally nominated exemplars. Education is about more than reaching targets. Accordingly we seek something richer, and in achieving this we are forced to disobey.

The premise of this book is that you can change things from the inside. If a whole system can't be reformed, infect what you can with positive initiatives. We are empowered to do this because we are educated, thinking professionals, capable of designing something better. Even at a micro-level our intervention still counts.

The viral infections I discuss here are drawn from my time in different parts of the education system, and all of them happened because I sensed that there was something better than what existed. They are not tales of wonder and revolution. I don't walk on water. However, each of them significantly changed something. They are based on three ideas about assessment. These are: the importance of self-evaluation, reducing the impact of marking, and the need for quality reporting.

Let's have a look at them.

self-evaluation

First up, some teachers don't really believe in marking. It has never made sense to them that you can replace the complexity of learning with an abstract grade. As a consequence, over time they design systems where learners appraise their own work and the work of others. We might understand this as a form of *self-control*. This is because if students can gain increasing insight into their learning, they can break the dependence on external, authority-based assessment.

In any education system in which I work, if I can't convince people that there might be something more effective than examination, I strategically disobey. I ascertain the minimal amount of testing required by those in 'authority', reluctantly tick those boxes and then set about infecting everything else with more effective approaches. Many teachers do this, in lots of different ways. Below are a few strategies that students have shown me that I have found useful.

Broadly, with the assistance of my classes, I design assessment formats that provide two layers of reflection. The first involves a personal critique by the learner. This is sometimes written but often it occurs in focused discussion. I ask students to outline perceived strengths and limitations in their work and suggest ways that any weaknesses might be addressed.

The second involves peer group critiques of work. These give an outsider viewpoint and also involve other learners in objective considerations of alternative solutions to an assignment their fellow students are also completing. Normally, small panels of peer reviewers are asked to critique three submissions that are not their own. They write a collective review. In return each student receives a panel assessment of their work.

It sounds very laudable, but of course it can be challenging to handle. Often students have become deeply dependent on marks. They go through a kind of withdrawal when they are asked to generate assessments that really count. They often prefer somebody else to take responsibility. They want rewards. It also takes a lot of work to get the system running smoothly, because you need very clear bottom lines about respect and expectations. You also have to negotiate with colleagues who may see you as not supporting a system that works comfortably for them and is the dominant approach of the institution inside which you are working.

I have found three ground rules useful in growing effective systems of self and peer evaluation.

- Only the person who has made the work can criticise the work.
- Others can offer positive comments, but, more importantly, they should ask analytical questions.
- Deadlines are absolute.

Let's look at these ideas individually:

Only the person who made the work can criticise the work

When a student presents what they have done, they are required to address two basic questions:

- What is effective about the solution and why?
- If I had the time again what would I change and why?

The analysis is expected to be critical, and when a statement is made, both students and the teacher will constantly ask, 'Why?' The process develops students' abilities in speaking articulately about their work before a group while growing their ability to critically analyse what they create. From their comments they are able to share information and techniques with each other that would otherwise remain sealed in the one-way communication between themselves and the teacher.

You can offer positive comments about another student's work, but you should also ask analytical questions

Initially it takes some effort to help students lift critique above congratulatory comments. While positive comments are useful, the skill that is really being developed is the ability to question somebody so that they dig deeper into issues affecting their work. This process often happens in small-group critiques where a person briefly presents and critiques their work, then opens the floor to peers. However, there are other approaches that have proved effective.

Sometimes, when small amounts of writing are submitted, we lay them out on tables and equip ourselves with sheets of paper.[28] Students spend the lesson reading along the line of submissions, and peer comments are written on the sheets and placed under the work. These sheets are taken home after the lesson and read by the student. Interestingly, people hang out for this process. For many students those sheets of paper represent, collectively, the most that has ever been written about their work. If the class is too big to do this successfully, then I design it like a peer review, where panels of two to three students assess and comment on the same number of designated, anonymous submissions. In this way, every piece of work receives two or three peer reviews.

The advantage, of course, is that students are thinking critically and evaluatively about not only their own work but also the work of others. This helps to grow communities of critical thinkers. It also allows us as teachers to consider (through observation) each student's increasing ability to analyse and critique.

Although this process began in a secondary-school classroom in the 1980s, I still use it today in developing peer-reviewing techniques with my postgraduate students. Normally, at the beginning of a year I give them three previously examined theses in their discipline and ask them to write an examiner's report for each. The theses contain significant strengths and normally one or two compromising flaws. Students bring drafts of their reports to a workshop, where they meet other candidates who have examined the same work. They are then asked to argue the merits and weaknesses of each thesis and justify their report on it. The debates are normally heated. The students encounter diverse approaches to how we might write about ideas. They expose the weakness of pretentious writing, under-researching and waffling. By critiquing and evaluating from the outset, they understand that their analysis of other people's work must be applied to the development of their own thesis.

Using this system changes a lot of priorities in teaching. Evaluation begins to take up a much larger proportion of time, but all of the hours spent at home with a pile of papers, poring over essays and allocating grades, are reduced. There are no averages or medians or standard deviations to calculate. The evaluations, because they are public, inform us both of the students' perception and of the process and subtlety that underpin their work. As educators we can question and find out much more than can be revealed through testing.

reducing the impact of marking

As an extension of this I do everything in my power to structure what I teach so that the allocation of marks is kept to a minimum. Accordingly, I try to treat anything that will be summatively assessed as a portfolio. This means I attempt to negotiate an approach where formative assessment takes up 90 per cent of a student's feedback, and at the end of the programme they submit a portfolio of work that they have been able to revisit and improve upon during the course. Thus, in the end only one mark is assigned and registered. It grades a composite body of work that has gone through a process of ongoing feedback and reworking.

At postgraduate level, in my honours and master's programmes, submitted work does not receive a fixed grade. It journeys through a spiral of experiences involving making, and self, peer and tutor questioning. Then the work is revisited and improved upon.

Each assignment folds into the next one. Writing can be reused, extended and refined. As a thesis or dissertation builds, the only purpose of assessment is to clarify and support the development of thinking.

At undergraduate level, assessment never appears as a list of grades for discrete tasks. Again, there is one grade, which is given at the end of the course. This is for a portfolio that normally contains a selection of three or four pieces and a reflective statement. In the statement the student describes and reviews their learning journey, critiques the outcomes of the study and lays the groundwork for thinking about method and methodology, which will be useful later in their academic career.

When I taught at secondary school I tried wherever possible to apply assessment innovations developed in disciplines like art, design and technology, which have historically used cumulative portfolios. I adapted the approach to a diverse range of subjects including English, social studies, biology and history. Where a school insisted on mid-year assessments, I asked that these be framed as formative and any mark 'required' for reporting purposes was delivered as a grade range. This sometimes took some negotiating. Where a school insisted on examinations or standardised testing and I couldn't negotiate anything else, I acquiesced but wrote a letter to the student and parents that offered a full context and description of what was really happening with the learning.

In primary and intermediate schools when I was forced to use standardised tests, I did everything I could to pare them back to a minimum. Again, I employed portfolios that were designed to be sent home with reports.[29] As a variation on this (and as a way of connecting self-evaluation to a longer-term form of self-reflection), I also experimented with what might be broadly referred to as 'time capsules'.

Let me explain. For nine years, in a metal box buried at the back of my property, I kept 32 of these. They were individually wrapped in bits of black plastic. They were created by 12-year-old students at an intermediate school where I was working who had designed and packaged them and handed them over, knowing that they wouldn't be due for delivery until their 20th birthday.

The capsules were eclectic affairs. They contained (in the student's estimation) their finest piece of writing from that year, their best artwork, their best project, photographs, mementos and, most significantly, a report to themselves. It was a secret letter that contained their predictions and the goals they hoped to achieve by the time they were 20. It also contained their opinions on a number of broad questions. These included:

- What do I believe happens to people when they die?
- Why do bad things sometimes happen to good people?
- What are the three most important things I will need to be happy when I am 20?

In addition to these reflections, most of the students included presents to themselves.

When it came time to track the students down they had become parents and executives and repairers of old cars. Some of them had married, moved overseas or gone to gaol. Telephone directories and electoral rolls were effective in locating only the minority of them. By the date of the last birthday in the class the capsules had been flown to Sweden and Israel, to flats and hospitals and to a house truck somewhere in the wilds of Fiordland.

But all of the documents found their way home. The letters I received during that year told of lives changed and driven down extraordinary paths, of dreams shattered and dreams fulfilled. But what was most important was that every person knew their capsule was coming. Every student remembered sealing the document nine years before and every student waited for its arrival.

Occasionally, in the years prior to their release, I'd receive a card at Christmas, tentatively recalling the reports and reminding me that the person was still there and wondering if the capsule was in existence. When it finally came time to dig them up, I confess I felt a bit worried. The capsules had gone mouldy, but when they were opened the contents were fortunately still intact. (Since then I have discovered the trouble-free nature of bank safety deposit boxes.)

The time capsule was an important idea because it made bridges in people's lives. It wasn't a collection of marks: it was a child's self-assessment of themselves, communicated to the adult they would become. It was a document that bridged time. It let people tell themselves about who they were as children and it used examples of their work to illustrate it. By putting what they produced in context with their beliefs and opinions, it became a creative and highly personal way of reporting.

quality reporting

More recently the idea of time capsules has been replaced by something more immediate. At the end of each year I now give gifts. This practice has a long tradition in education: historically many teachers have given and received small tokens of appreciation at the end of a year spent with their students. At the university where I work the gifts I give are small potted herbs accompanied by a handwritten letter. This letter tries to describe the kind of learner I have experienced during our time together. Each student's learning is linked metaphorically to lore surrounding the plant, or to something specific about the way it grows. In giving such a gift I try to negate the authority of a mark that will eventually arrive from some external party. In some cases I know these plants won't make it through the summer holidays; they will die on the window-sill of an unkempt flat, or they will be planted in conditions that would threaten the survival of a radioactive cockroach. But in other cases they grow and years later I hear back from people. I go to their weddings and attend the births of their babies and they remember these small things.

This is a form of 'reporting' that surfaces as a consequence of learning together. It does not explain a mark. It accepts that we are not learning information and skills but using these things to develop as human beings. I try to make any feedback personal, and connected not just to the submitted work but also to the learner and the uniqueness of their journey. I take a lot of time to listen, write to and talk with students. They know I think about them – not just about what they produce but also about them as people. It has taken many years for me to learn how important it is to do such things.

letters home

The origin of this approach surfaced 30 years ago when I was teaching in a small King Country college where I was trying to work out a way of reporting on learning more effectively. This was because the school report template only had space for a mark, a class ranking and a small rectangle for entering a few words like 'Could do better'. When I explained that I would like to write more fully on the students' learning, I was asked not to continue my comments on to the back of the report sheet because it was felt that in so doing I was pressuring my colleagues into doing the same. I was not being a good team player.

But, you know, it is very difficult to sum up the complexity of somebody's learning in a 10 x 30mm rectangle. I didn't want to upset my colleagues, so I took to writing discrete letters. These were given out on the same day as the report, in class, quietly, one to each student. The letters talked about how I thought they were learning, how they appeared to solve problems, and the unique nature of their progress and aspirations. Sometimes the letters were poetic, sometimes tender, sometimes critical, but always appreciative.

Interestingly, when the ritual of the report evening arrived, it was these pieces of paper that parents brought with them. They were proud that somebody commented on their child's acerbic wit or creative excuse making, or their ability to sense anxiety in others and help before anyone else noticed. Marks and grade point averages do not engender such things. What matters is the care one human being takes to talk about another.

I still write in such depth, be it for a class of 30 students or for the supervision of a single postgraduate candidate. Because my teaching is strategically cleared of fragmented assessment tasks and unnecessary marking, I have more time to listen to and talk with the students with whom I work. Such approaches are better than a B+ or 'achieved'. They tell people that they matter.

disproportion

I do not claim that these approaches to assessment are transferable. They are not a template for a working alternative. They are idiosyncratic, but also indicative of things I see all around me when I watch talented teachers make space for more humane and insightful approaches to assessment. They are disobedient interventions in a system that has lost its sense of priority.

I do not believe that testing has no place in schools, but its current, disproportionate prominence is damaging. It has filled too many spaces and priorities, so that teachers, in a scramble to meet testing requirements, have little time to develop deeply reflective learning environments. A friend of mine teaching in a small rural school once summed up her predicament this way: 'We spend so much time weighing the sheep that we have no time to feed it.'

While the image may cause us to smile, the reality doesn't. Yet despite the cramping nature of too much testing and the prosaic teaching models it reinforces, certain teachers continue to systematically disobey dominant practice in order to transform learning by using assessment as an informal, diagnostic tool that is embedded in a process of observing, discussing, co-creating and listening. They can describe what is emerging, consider what they encounter against a range of social and personal contexts, and then edge their way intuitively forward. This kind of assessment is not a ruler. It is not absolute and is rarely recordable. But it is the foundation of evaluation, and certainly the most active agent in understanding student progress.

The problem is that such immersive forms of assessment are rarely rewarded outside of the intimate relationship established between the learner and the teacher. In our mistaken assumption that learning produces a valid, measurable product we end up rewarding only that which can be turned into performance. This is a senseless and toxic situation. It elevates measurement above knowing, and no effective education system can develop from such a position.

* * *

PART FOUR
PASSION

someone who counts

A few months ago I was giving a keynote address at a conference. There were about 150 teachers in the room and all had given up time from their holidays to be there. Although they represented a wide cross-section of educators, what impressed me was the generous way in which they shared intimate experiences and teaching experiments with each other. Nobody was grandstanding, and the conference was focused on finding ways to enhance relationships between students and curriculum. In my talk I was discussing what actually causes change in people; as everyone had some paper in front of them, I asked them to write down the name of a teacher in their past who had significantly transformed their lives for the better. On a conservative calculation, by the time they completed their bachelor's degree they had been taught by 47 different educators, so they had a substantial body of experience to consider. They were asked to choose only one teacher. With no further prompting each person wrote down a name. Then I asked them to visualise that person and to write down a sentence that summarised why they had such a transformative effect on their life.

After they had briefly discussed the reason for selecting this teacher with the person next to them, I asked them to stand up if they had chosen that teacher because of his or her ability to assess against curriculum objectives. Nobody stood up. So I asked them to stand up if the reason was related to how the teacher used new technologies to disseminate information. Nobody stood up. Then I asked them to stand up if the reason was somehow tied to the humanity of that person, to the way they took time to touch the essence of them as a learner and an individual. Slowly, sometimes sheepishly 149 people stood up: a whole room, bar one woman, who later said she was unable to recall any teacher who had a positive influence on her.

The teachers looked around themselves. It was an extraordinary depiction of something we all know very well. Profound teaching, transformative teaching, does not draw its essence from curriculum structure or tools of dissemination or planning and marking objectives, but from the quality of a human being. Despite the rhetoric of accountability, it is the nature of humanity that lies at the centre of transformative learning and teaching. If you want human beings to function well, you have to give them space to do so. You have to trust them and their authenticity.

the intimate practitioner

Many educational theorists have highlighted the importance of personal relationships and teacher agency in learning.[30] Even the Ministry of Education's Curriculum Stocktake back in 2002 found that 'quality teaching makes more difference to student outcomes than any other factor'.[31] What the stocktake may have naively missed, however, is the fact that the quality of relationships formed by teachers with a group of students affects something far more profound than a collection of outcomes. It affects the way that people will continue to learn and their development as human beings.

It is impossible for effective teachers to be objective constructions, a step removed from the intimacy of the students with whom they work. Ivan Snook puts it this way:

A teacher can rarely hide behind an impersonal role, concealing her personal values, beliefs and attitudes. Locked up with perhaps 30 vigorous and inquisitive young people, her every weak spot is well known, her passing moods well noted, her personality constantly analyzed. Similarly she comes to know her students very closely; their character, personality, beliefs and values are out in the open for the sensitive teacher.[32]

However, much political handwringing over teaching undervalues the wealth of experience and insight that students and teachers bring to the dynamic of learning. Emotional experience, intuition, inspiration, courage and passion are immeasurable. To accommodate such qualities, any system of learning has to accept as a premise that all participants are trading beyond experience. The starting blocks cannot be the same, and any expectation of comparable, standardised performance is illogical. Learning's potential to occur is hugely enhanced when the human being, rather than the outcome, is placed at the centre of the process. The power of a teacher lies not so much in their ability to disseminate knowledge or meet outcomes as in their ability to transform understanding. Let me give you an example.

Miss Jull

When I was 15 I had an English teacher called Miss Jull. Miss Jull was the senior mistress of Te Awamutu College and most people lived in terror of her. She had jet-black hair and long fingers that constantly played at her throat. When she talked to an assembly of adolescents she could chill the auditorium. Yet Miss Jull was immensely human. On the desk in her class she always kept a small vase of fresh flowers and it shone like a light in the beige world of curriculum English. With her we covered comprehension exercises and old examination papers, all of which we have forgotten, but 40 years later her poetry still endures.

Some days Miss Jull would stand at the front of the class and read. There was an array of authors from William Wordsworth to Sylvia Plath, from Carl Sandburg to George Santayana. When she read to you she could make your blood run cold; it felt like she was telling you something immensely personal and private, something about a world that was too intimate for a classroom.

I will always remember the day she read us Wilfred Owen's *Dulce et Decorum Est*. She stood over by the window and told us the story of a war. In her fingers she held a blue book, but she seemed hardly to glance at it. If you closed your eyes you could almost hear the bombs dropping in the distance. But even more memorable than the power of the words was the fact that as she struggled towards the closing verses her voice began to waver. We sat there in silence, a class of Te Awamutu fifth formers, and watched as this paragon of stoic control began to cry at the words of a dead poet.

In all my dreams, before my helpless sight,
He plunges at me, guttering, choking, drowning.

In the legend that circulated around the school, we were convinced this was the story of Miss Jull's lover who had gone away to war and never returned; if Wilfred Owen hadn't actually written the poem about him then the words obviously brought back poignant memories. We imagined her standing at the local railway station watching hopelessly as the soldiers bundled from their trains and into the arms of their fiancées. Laughing and hugging, they would reel off the platform and disappear into the night. But Miss Jull would always be standing there alone, left on the concrete with a bunch of wilted flowers and an old blue poetry book balanced delicately between her fingers.

It was tragic and wonderful, and as far from the truth as it was possible to get. But, by God, it was a magnificent story and she was a magnificent teacher. I can never read Wilfred Owen without seeing her in the shadows, waiting. The wonderful thing is that her passion still exists. She is replicated in schools up and down the country. She is the music teacher who turns up to discuss the compositions of Rimsky-Korsakov in a bumblebee suit, or the guy who jumps on the science desks to demonstrate nuclear reaction, or the storyteller who teaches German culture by weaving ancient legends in a darkened classroom. These are the teachers who leave the marks. They are the people who don't always have their lesson plans done, who have to fudge the odd 'requirement', who spend large chunks of their holidays gathering resources, and who bore people at parties with inexhaustible stories about the kids with whom they are working. They are the quality in each of us that celebrates learning through its passion for people. And they are the most valuable and untrusted resource in the education system.

the marshmallow cocoon

It has been my experience that passionate teachers generally live their professional lives in a state of productive questioning, renegotiating the mundane and the accepted. They are not submissive to authority because they have a natural propensity to disobey. But this is not disrespectful. We trust them because we experience their faith in us. They are also often excessive in their apportioning of time, so it is their *enthusiasm* rather than their strategic efficiency that drives us to learn so richly under their guidance.

'Enthusiasm' is a beautiful word. It is derived from the Greek *en theos*, meaning inner god. A teacher possessed of an inner god might in contemporary language be described as self-actualised or inspired by something internal. Such teachers know themselves well enough to take risks with their own learning and that of others. They understand that no knowledge is safe and that reducing learning to a cocoon of reliable inputs and responses to prescribed success indicators undermines what it is to think. The teachers who become transformative are those who take us beyond the marshmallow realm of the safely pre-imagined.

The transformative nature of positive disobedience lies at the base of change. This is why questioning is so important in education, and also why protecting ideas or practices by elevating the idea of safety beyond its role of limiting debilitating damage is misguided. Learning is not safe, because thinking is not safe.

Excessive preoccupation with the idea of 'safety' in education often leads to a kind of cocooning that operates on diverse levels. It can be seen in coddled notions of 'safe' playgrounds where behaviour is consciously redesigned or monitored so it operates inside prescribed limitations. While protecting children physically and emotionally is important, such care requires balancing against their need as young human beings to explore new situations with curiosity and increasing confidence.[33]

Mark A. Reinecke, the chair of psychology and child development at Northwestern University in Illinois, has noted that play environments are 'microcosms of a child's world, where the lessons learned reverberate through their lives'. This idea has been developed by a growing number of writers,[34] but it was famously unpacked in 2011 by Ellen Sandseter and Leif Kennair in an article in the *Journal of Evolutionary Psychology*. Here, they noted that young children naturally develop fears of certain stimuli, such as heights and strangers. These fears protect children from situations for which they are not yet mature enough to cope. Risky play is a method they have of moving beyond these anxieties as they mature. The exhilarating, positive emotions experienced when they conquer these fears reinforce their coping skills and incrementally strengthen their ability to master age-adequate challenges as these arise in their lives. Cocooning the world of physical and social play limits children's access to such occurrences, which means they do not experience these small victories and consequently can end up still nurturing fears inappropriate to their age and physical skill levels long after other children have developed more advanced coping mechanisms. Put more bluntly, when young people are over-cocooned, their development – physically and psychologically – is stunted because they never develop the experiences of failure and achievement that move them forward as human beings.

If cocooning can limit our ability to develop physically, it can also operate on intellectual and social levels. Learning environments can be consciously massaged into a marshmallow state where students' interrogation of the socialising forces that shape them is circumvented. Such environments can end up inhibiting their development as critical, enabled, adult thinkers. This is a serious issue when we realise that damaging social constructs such as fundamentalism, uncritical allegiance and social prejudice all depend on individuals learning not to question.

The need in teaching to activate a questioning and open engagement with the intimately experienced does not absolve educators of the need to consider the consequences of damaging practice.[35] In fact our decision to move out of the safety of the marshmallow cocoon shines a stronger light on the values we employ in teaching and the consequences of our actions. This is because as we deal more openly with lived experience, discrepancies in our professional and personal practice become more pronounced. As a consequence, we are actually called upon more frequently to reflect on, explain and justify our choices.

the main street experiment

We all know examples of teaching that moved us out of the marshmallow cocoon. It is what stays with us because it is what is most likely to have transformed us as a human being. Such educative experiences rely on the quality of the teacher and the trust they develop with their students. When this relationship is used to turn learning into an embodied experience it becomes profound. However, when we choose to pursue this kind of teaching we can find ourselves confronted by unstable things like intensity, intimate revelation and conflicting values. Our traditional role as guardian of the parameters is extended. Risks are taken and we move increasingly into a realm of vulnerability similar to what is experienced by our students.

If this sounds a little abstract, let me illustrate. I used to teach social studies to 11-year-olds. Every year we covered the curriculum using books and photographs and television documentaries. My colleagues and I thought we were doing a good job. Our students produced brightly coloured projects that demonstrated how well they'd researched, and they made posters and maps and met the requirements of the department scheme. The success indicators were all ticked off.

Among the topics that we covered each year was a unit on prejudice. When the topic arrived we'd examine the Blacks in America or the Jews in Warsaw or the plight of women in contemporary society. We were well resourced and politically correct and, short of actually stopping a Ku Klux Klan meeting or derailing a train on its way to the death camps, the class felt assured by the end of the year that they had learnt something new and become socially sensitive to the issue.

At school at that time we had a girl with a cleft lip. Her name was Marty and she was partly deaf. She wore her jacket with its hood pulled well down over her face and when she talked to you – which wasn't often – she spoke with a speech impediment. It was difficult to understand what she was saying. Marty didn't mix much with other kids; usually she would spend her lunchtimes over by the basketball courts, on a corner seat, reading.

In our social studies class the kids felt sorry for her. When they talked about it they said it was sad that she was left out of things and that the school should provide more activities at lunchtime so she could become involved. They regretted that she was an outsider – but they didn't hang around with her or invite her to their parties or ask her to be on their sports teams. She would never be one of their partners at the school socials. When the joke circulated, *Why did Marty's dog jump off the cliff?* 'You would too if your name was Noof neef noofie*, they all laughed.

The reference to her speech impediment was savage. When I questioned them about it, they said that the joke wasn't funny and was prejudiced, and that it was a group of boys who were telling it. They knew the right responses; they could fluster themselves into poses of indignation and speak out loudly about such humour being inappropriate and a form of bullying. All the same, everybody knew the joke.

In our neat urban existence we were pampered philanthropists. It was easy to deal with prejudice because it remained an intellectual issue. Here, nobody spat at you or refused to serve you in a shop or left you sitting over by the basketball courts. We were white and bright and very socially sensitive, and when we studied prejudice we always did a good job of it. That's why, one year when the unit of work began, I threw out all the resources.

On the first day of the topic we all arranged to arrive at school dressed up as 'nerds'. It was the early 1980s and the term had recently become popular. In the briefing the day before it sounded like fun. We were going to be outcasts in our own school culture, and to celebrate we would have a bad-taste party together, with green cakes and purple ginger beer and sandwiches with crazy fillings. To these kids nerds and bad taste were conflated ideas. Everybody thought it was a good plan. But in truth it wasn't going to be quite as innocent as it looked.

The class arrived in a plethora of atrocities, from pink socks with sandals, to underpants worn over jeans; from bow ties and running shorts to lime green hair. We gathered around the classroom door, laughing and shouting and waving out to each other. But when the bell went and they got ready to go inside, I suggested that we change the plan. I proposed that we walk into town and take part in an experiment.

There was some nervous laughter at first and a few crazy hats disappeared into back pockets, but with the assurance that the trip would take the whole day and the group would be released from their other classes, their apprehension quickly dwindled. We set off.

When we got into town we sat down on a traffic island at the north end of the main street. The three parents who turned up had decked themselves out in leathers and lipstick and eight-inch pumps and the kids shrieked with amazement as they strutted across the street to join us. Everybody was high on the adrenalin and the novelty of it all, and they squealed with laughter when cars drove past tooting their horns.

But the excitement quickly turned to something more serious when they were told that the experiment wasn't going to be a party on a traffic island. We talked for a little while about the kinds of people who become ordinary victims of prejudice and what it's like to be vulnerable in a place like the centre of your own home town. I explained that, dressed as we were, we were going to walk down the two kilometres of main street, stop in at a shop and politely purchase something, and then, when we got to the far end of town, we'd go down to the river for a picnic.

There were three ground rules underpinning the expedition. The first two would be easy to follow. We all had to keep the same clothes on but were *not* to consciously provoke any response; we were simply going to walk harmlessly and unobtrusively through the city. Second, none of us was to deviate from the set route, even if it became uncomfortable or we felt embarrassed. What we had to be aware of was *how it actually felt* to be an object of prejudice, and to try and remember *how people react* to someone who is different.

At this point the class was still enthusiastic, although perhaps a little more reserved. Some of the kids were whispering to each other and quickly sorting out who was walking down with whom and which group was going first. Then came the third ground rule. I told them that they would have to do the experiment on their own. They would need to leave, *one at a time*, at two-minute intervals, walking on alternate sides of the street, and would not be allowed to make contact with anybody else in the class.

The group went quiet.

There was some shuffling and two lots of coloured hair began to disappear up under hats. Shane looked down at the underpants that he had put on over his jeans and asked what would happen if he got arrested. The responding laughter was nervous. I looked at the group.

'Why are you frightened?' I asked.

Sharon glanced up. 'Because people will laugh at us. They'll think that we're losers.'

'Why are you afraid of that?'

Her look was incredulous. 'Oh come on!' she said.

'No. Seriously. Why are we so afraid of being thought of as a "loser"? Why are we sitting here, shuffling around, trying to change our costumes so they don't look so excessive, so we won't stand out?'

Several kids froze in the process of adjustment.

'Why are we doing that? Can a Black man do that? Or a Korean tourist? Can you make prejudice go away by changing your costume?'

There was silence. I looked at them. They were obviously worried. They sat around on the grass in their fluoro braces and lacquered hair and looked very vulnerable. Then Mark asked, 'What if we get beaten up?' A few kids glanced sideways at each other.

'Do you think that could happen?' I asked.

'If you were on your own,' he said.

'Why do you think you'd get beaten up?'

He fumbled with his braces for a moment and then looked up at me. 'For being different.'

I glanced at the class. 'For being different. Do you think that could happen? Here in Hamilton, in the main street? Do you think people get beaten up for being different?'

They frowned.

When the first person set off we waved goodbye and watched

as she disappeared into the amble of mid-morning shoppers. The kids had been assured that if anything really untoward happened they could walk back to find the next student or stand by a pedestrian crossing for a patrolling parent's car, and if they didn't feel like going they could stay behind and get a lift down to the picnic site with one of the fathers who had also turned up. But there were no takers.

When we met up again at the park there were stories galore. There was laughter and shouting and cheers of encouragement. Only a few of the kids had been able to hold to the ground rules. Most of them had begun to feel embarrassed or anxious and had waited around outside a shop until they could meet up with one of their friends. Roger and Karl, two of the 'staunch' boys in the class, whipped down to the river bank and changed out of their costumes because the whole thing was silly and a waste of time, and somebody had called them a couple of poofs.

For Ingrid and Sarah the crowd's reaction had been more subtle. As they walked down the street everyone had averted their eyes. People, they discovered, had a way of pointing at you by deliberately pretending that you didn't exist. Shane still had his underpants stretched over the outside of his jeans. He'd been stared at and called a wanker and told to 'Fuck off!' at a takeaway, when he stopped to buy himself a Moro bar. The class was in awe of him. There was a new kind of respect for anybody who braved KFC in a pair of high-heeled shoes and his dad's Y-fronts.

As we ate our picnic we talked about the experiment and how it felt to be disapproved of or laughed at, or consciously ignored by people. Everybody had felt it, but what had hit the hardest weren't the stares and the odd insult, but the complete sense of being alone, the feeling of vulnerability and isolation and the awareness that you were being shut out of your own world.

That night they went home and wrote or drew or composed something that documented the reality of what had happened to them. Everybody did something. They showed up the next morning with poems, pictures, music and pages of writing. We covered the walls and talked about people in our society who face prejudice every day. They weren't dealing with abstracts now: they talked about being fat or your voice not breaking or having a mum who drinks and not being able to invite your friends around to stay overnight. They talked about *how* prejudice felt. Their discussions were quite unlike anything we'd ever experienced before: intense and unpredictable, making links between ideas and private worlds.

When we finally looked at the harassment of the Jews in the thirties, they began to understand. There were no horror pictures of piles of glasses or open graves, just a photograph of a little girl at a broken window. Instead of condemning, the kids were frowning and nodding and talking about how she must have felt. They talked about why sticking around your friends or family would be important for support and how if you made people afraid by using prejudice it's much harder for them to fight back.

I kept one piece of writing from that class. I found it in my bag one afternoon after I got home from school. It was a letter written by one of the girls who had aroused a lot of admiration because she had completed the Main Street experiment without compromising any of the ground rules. It made me understand the subtle places that this form of learning can touch. The letter appears as she wrote it and I use it here with her permission.

Dear Welby,

I am writing this because I am a liar and I want to tell you about what happened. When we went into town, I didn't walk down the street like everybody thought I did. When I was out of sight,

I went behind a shop and changed out of my costume and snuck down along the river bank. I didn't do it because I wanted to cheat, but because I was scared. When people looked at me, I wanted to curl up and die because I knew what they were thinking. You knew when you walked past them, that they were looking back at you and saying things. I tried to pull my hat right down low so they wouldn't see my face, but even that doesn't hide you. Most of all I was scared that someone would recognise me.

When I got back into my own clothes, I looked at my costume on the ground and it made me think of a skin, the sort of thing that other people can't take off. I thought of how I pulled my hat down over my face and how Marty sits on the seats at lunchtime, hidden under her hood. I never knew before. If that's what it's like for me, for ten minutes, what must it be like for her, for her whole life?

It made me feel horrible.
I hope you're not angry at me.

Love
Belinda.

What do you say? The only way into the hearts of these kids was potentially unsafe, but a kind of intimacy surfaced that transformed the rest of the year for us. A week earlier I had co-created the idea with three sets of parents who I knew would be willing to help and would keep a discreet but watchful eye on what unfolded. The obvious point is that such an initiative was risky, but it was carefully planned and its potential variables had been considered and discussed.

Educatively, what became more important than the event itself was its debriefing. This was designed so that the students' embodied experiences could become a vehicle for understanding wider social issues. The discussions, reflections and creative work they generated went beyond reading and responding. They drew on lived experience, and in so doing entered the realm of transformation.

accountability

Historically such responsive approaches to learning have sat more comfortably with New Zealand liberal education models that grew out of Peter Fraser's and Clarence Beeby's visions of the 1940s. Today's concern that education should meet the needs of mark-based accountability has skewed the 'teachable moment' spaces that once offered educators comparatively more flexibility. In the current climate of education we often find ourselves singing the praises of the 'teachable moment' and 'student centredness', but we are hard pressed to find room to pursue such approaches in a meaningful way.

There is a reason for this. When in 1993 the New Zealand Curriculum Framework abolished syllabuses in favour of mission statements, it introduced unit standards that divided learning into discrete components, each with its own achievement objective. It established seven essential learning areas for pupils from Years 1 to 10, and clearly shifted curriculum policy from, in the Ministry of Education's words, 'a focus on content to a policy based on outcomes'.[36] This increasing prioritising of measurability and accountability did not develop unquestioned. Since the framework was first considered, educationalists such as Ivan Snook, Joce Jesson, Roger Openshaw, Peter Roberts, Jane Robertson and Anne-Marie O'Neil have continued to express concerns that New Zealand has developed a business model of education that places too much emphasis on performing and measuring. This, they suggest, has occurred at the cost of connected and inter-related understanding. In this environment the generation of measurable artefacts and performances has gradually become more valued than the process of learning. This may be very good if we understand education in terms of performance and its indicators, but we might ask, 'Does this systematised, measurable and demarcating paradigm value learning, or merely nominated performances of it?'

fear and hope

Over time I have come to understand learning as something essentially emotional that reaches far beyond measurable cognitive function. I believe that all learners navigate learning subjectively, and that the relationship between what we learn and who we are is indivisible. As a way of dealing with this I sometimes imagine that, as learners, we carry a creature on each shoulder. Unlike the archetypal conscience angel and tempting devil of the cartoon strips, these figures are hope and fear. When we enter a learning experience we hope that we will understand, we hope that we will become more capable, and we hope that our investment in risk, time and resources will pay off. Moreover, we hope that others will admire us for what we achieve. But we are also afraid. We are scared that we may squander a great deal of effort to no avail; we are afraid that we may be humiliated and that our limitations might be displayed for everyone to see. Carrying these two agents on our shoulders, we move forward into new territory.

By thinking about learning as emotional, and understanding it as something motivated by hope but constrained by fear, we are able to bring learners into very intimate contact with what they learn. Here they draw on higher levels of personal relevance and passionate commitment that equip them with the tenacity they need to negotiate things when times get difficult. With these elements they can move beyond the abstract rewards of marks or grades to higher levels of intrinsic relevance. But more than this, when we are emotionally involved with what we learn, we come closer to the potential for transformation. In almost every case of transformative learning I have encountered, both risk (overcoming fear) and passion have been fundamental elements. The outcomes of such learning are not uniformly predictable, but lives change as a consequence.

Perhaps three examples across 40 years of teaching might serve to illustrate. In each of these cases something shifted for both the learner and the people in the environment surrounding them. All of them involve emotion and learning in a profoundly integrated relationship.

Elizabeth

Elizabeth was seven when I taught her. She lived with her mother. Each Monday she would bounce into the classroom at 8am with a small bunch of flowers blazing like fire between her fingers. There were marigolds and pansies and sometimes exotic specimens for which I had no name. She told me these were 'Princess flowers' that her mum had picked and I was to put them in water with a teaspoon of sugar. I was later to discover that she had in fact pinched them from local people's gardens on her way to school. However, in our shared innocence she would busy herself scrubbing dried paint off a jar from the art cupboard and I would locate the bowl of ant-infested sugar I had salvaged from the staffroom. I would ask her where she thought the flowers would look the most beautiful.

Elizabeth loved anything bright. Her desk was full of crayons and old chocolate wrappers, and she was wont to occasionally 'relocate' shiny things from the nature table. She was also an avid reader. She read *The Hungry Lambs*, *Boat Day*, *The Donkey's Egg* and *Stars in the Sky*. These were the graduated early-reader books that constituted the generic diet of 1970s New Zealand education. Elizabeth's reading age was far beyond what you might expect for a seven-year-old. I remember one day asking her why she liked books so much and she said a curious thing: that reading 'took her away'. It seemed an innocent enough comment at the time.

At the end of our first six weeks working together I sent home a glowing report to her mother. It praised her daughter's progress and commitment. However, I was surprised when nobody turned up to parent interviews two days later. When I asked my colleagues if they knew what might have happened, one of them took me aside and explained the situation. Elizabeth's mum was back in prison. She was a habitual heroin addict and the child's home life was a series of repeated rescues and emergency placements in foster care. Last year Elizabeth had been hospitalised twice due to beatings and neglect, and she was currently living with a family who were about to leave the district and couldn't take her with them.

The next morning Elizabeth brought me more flowers and took a new book from the library. Rearranging the cushions on the sofa she prepared to read me a story. I sat down as I did most days, and she cuddled up against me. She had chosen the hardest book in the Learning to Read series. It was called *Sliding and Flying*. Her reading was beautiful, full of wonder and expression, but the words weren't written on the page. She 'read' me a story about a princess who lived with her beautiful mother in a golden castle. They had a garden that grew magical flowers and she had her own special dog. Her story went beyond my experience. She shared a world that could take her away, and while she read, she reached up and draped my arm around her shoulder. I looked down at her, so small and full of magic, and in that moment I think I felt my heart break for the very first time.

Joey

I supervised Joey at university and at his request I am using his real name. Joey enrolled in a master's degree in documentary filmmaking because he wanted to become a director. Despite being talented, he didn't see himself as more gifted than the other students with whom he worked. He was bright, personable and dedicated. He wanted to make films about ordinary people and his ambition should have been a smooth road forward.

However, in the months leading up to beginning his thesis he contacted me with the news that he had been diagnosed with nephrotic syndrome. Over the next few months I watched as he wrestled with a potentially terminal kidney disease. Despite the diagnosis he returned to Manila to shoot footage for a documentary he wanted to make about the poor kids who lived on the streets where he grew up. When he returned to New Zealand he was very ill. His muscles had deteriorated to the extent that he could barely walk; he was swollen and often collapsed with weakness. In the end he was hospitalised. Through all of this he continued to develop his thesis.

When I talked with him about taking time out he said that he couldn't. He was frightened but also determined. At 21 he didn't want his life to be over. He told me that he had ideas about a new form of documentary making and these were something he had to hold on to. I remember visiting him in hospital one afternoon. He was housed in one of those bleached linoleum wards that was full of signs and whispered efficiency. When I popped my head around the door he looked up and smiled. He had his computer on his lap and he surreptitiously tapping away at a draft of his thesis. He wasn't supposed to be doing this, but he knew he could hide his laptop under his sheet if the nurses arrived. He was excited about the fact that he had found a new way of editing material so that his documentaries would be more lyrical.

Over the years I have supervised many master's and PhD theses, and each journey has been different, but Joey's was unique. Through him I learned about the sustaining nature of passion. I witnessed the ferocity of hope, and the need sometimes to hold on tightly to living ideas. I also learned about the look in someone's eyes when they decide to live.

When it was submitted, Joey's thesis was extraordinary. When you read it you got the sense that it was written by somebody much older, not because of its language but because of the attitudes and insights that permeated its thinking. The documentaries he made as part of his study were officially selected for numerous international film festivals and won an array of awards. His thesis passed with first-class honours. Slowly, with determination, he had learned how to grip the few lifelines available to him, and one of them had been his study.

Joey makes films and music videos now, and he shoots material for a plethora of large organisations. If you passed him in the street you would never know how the strength of passion held him together over his weeks in hospital. In an early chapter of his thesis he wrote,

> *When you face the possibility of death in your early twenties, many values reformat. Certain fundamental ideas prioritise. Love, support and aspiration become more than euphoric virtues, you realise that they are fundamental to survival and to understanding what it is to live a fulfilling life.*[37]

His thesis was called 'Aspire'. His films told lyrical, hopeful stories of kids who assembled kites from old plastic bags and whose entertainment was a tin can tossed into a chalk circle. The films are full of colour and human detail, and they tell us about learning on very deep levels. They are not tick-box performances; they have passion and empathy, and reveal profound insights into what it is to be a human being.

Edward

I worked with Edward back in the 1990s. At 15 he wanted to be a dancer, but you would never know it if you watched him strutting around the tuck shop or talking to his mates, because he kept his lessons a secret. On most days he would arrive at school early so he could score some breakfast. Such meals weren't a certainty with him because he spent a lot of time away from home.

Edward loved music. From Rachmaninov to Jane's Addiction, he delighted in its imagery. He wrote books of lyrics and filled sketchpads with sets and backdrops for his songs. He said that writing and dancing your own music was the closest thing you got to being God. And yet in class his passion never surfaced. When the bell rang he simply dissolved into the background, slipped through the hoops and produced only what was required to reach the minimum standard. He'd learnt that by doing this he could avoid any unwanted attention.

Edward had contempt for schooling. He didn't see out the year, but I will always remember the presentation of his last school assignment. He called us into the hall, where he had blacked out the stage and set a solitary spotlight down onto the curtains. We knew that he had designed a self-directed performance of a piece of contemporary dance music, but I guess few of us were expecting much. He'd been absent for almost two weeks and had spent a lot of his previous time in class explaining how uninterested he was in anything to do with school. So it was with surprise that we watched when the curtains opened and an extraordinary set emerged from the darkness. It was made entirely of huge photocopies of snarling dogs. They hung from the ceiling at discordant angles and the mirrors set in their eyes reflected the light.

We sat there in silent amazement and watched as slowly, from out of the darkness, the music began to filter. It was a drum and a glockenspiel, dubbed over with the sounds of voices and heart-beats. He had mixed it on a friend's audio system. It was a synergy of sculpture and sound that few of us had expected. We waited …

Then from the shadows at the edge of the set there emerged a small figure, dressed in a balaclava and black jeans. He began to weave his way between the hangings, advancing and retreating in the light like a cautious animal. He was fluid and supple, fright-ened and aware – jumping on cue and flinching at the sound of a bell. This was his music. He had composed it himself. He was dancing the Ballet of Pavlov's Dogs.

When the presentation was over nobody clapped. We were awestruck. He came back down into the group and talked briefly about what he'd done – the strengths and weaknesses of the set and the improvements he could have made to the music. He didn't mention the dance.

Nobody knew quite how to respond. The performance had been extraordinary. There wasn't much you could say. It was out of context for someone whose fostered identity had revolved around scabbing drinks off people at the tuck shop and reading his name out on the detention lists. The performance had been a door to a part of him that few in the group had suspected. When eventually some of the people tried to ask him about the dance he brushed them aside. He said it was just bullshit that he'd just slapped together at the last minute. He said that it didn't matter.

The next morning I arrived at school at 7.30am. Edward was sitting on the steps. There had been a frost and he was shivering. He'd slept the night in one of those recycled clothing bins they put in the corner of supermarket carparks. I opened up and he put on the jug and made us both a cup of coffee. We talked for a while, sitting there on opposite sides of the table, and he told me again what a load of crap the performance had been; how it had meant nothing to him and how gullible he had found the group to be in their analysis. I watched him as he gulped down the last of his drink and put his mug down on to the table. He told me he was leaving school.

He looked up at me again, just to make sure that I understood the truth of what he was saying. 'It was nothing,' he said, '... the dance.'

I nodded.

And then he started crying.

In the movies this would be a point of denouement. Truth and revelation would sweep across the scene and the world would come right. But they didn't, because this is life and Edward left school that afternoon. He left town too. He closed the door on his schooling with one heartbreaking insight into the young man he was and I never heard from him again.

Nobody ever tells you when you become a teacher that you will encounter situations like these, and that the more loved and trusted you are, the higher the chance is that such incidents will occur. I think this happens because over time kids recognise some teachers as strong and compassionate, not in the mode of a carefully prescribed set of parameters, but as human beings who are honest about their own limitations and accepting of the flaws in others.

affection

But absorbing ideas emotionally and working with the effects of this relies on a certain level of intimacy, and intimacy is something we have learned to be professionally afraid of. When in 1998 the New Zealand Educational Institute (NZEI), which represents staff at primary schools, early education centres and special education centres, issued a code of practice on physical contact, it surfaced at a time of high-level anxiety surrounding such physical contact between adults and young children. This was partly a consequence of the moral panic that in 1993 contributed to the conviction of Peter Ellis for his supposed sexual abuse of children at the Christchurch Civic Childcare Centre.

In 1993 Peter Ellis, a preschool teacher, was controversially found guilty of 16 counts of sexual offences involving seven children. Despite the absence of adult eyewitnesses and physical evidence, he was sentenced to 10 years' imprisonment. Although eligible for parole from March 1998, Ellis refused to appear before the board, stating that he would stay in prison if accepting parole required him to admit to a crime that he did not commit. He was eventually released in February 2000 after serving almost seven years in prison.

This case pre-empted a significant shift in education risk management despite the fact that no research had shown an increase in child abuse between teachers and pupils at the time.[38] The 1998 code warned that touching could be misconstrued and it placed teachers at the risk of assault or indecency allegations. It said staff should explain to children why a teacher withdrew from them, and it was clear that any physical contact with children represented a professional risk. The code listed inappropriate contact situations and advised all teachers to avoid physical contact if possible. Teachers were also advised to avoid being alone with a child, comforting them with a hug, leaning over them closely at a desk, holding their hands or showing signs of congratulatory affection.

This anxiety engendered a markedly different climate from post-World War Two classroom environments where physical touch between teachers and pupils was an accepted and expected part of developing well-rounded individuals. Up until the early

1980s it was common to see teachers on playground duty with a teacup in one hand and a group of kids holding on to the other, or to pass a classroom and watch children cuddled affectionately up against a teacher's legs while she was reading to them. Affection was normal. It was part of the way teachers modelled nurturing relationships and created emotional security in their classrooms. If a child hurt himself in the playground, he would get a cuddle and reassurance; if she was playing, she might get a piggy back; if children were having trouble with a problem, their teacher might hunker down on the floor beside them and help them explore it. Touch and learning were part of a normal, trust-oriented world.

However, as educators began to rethink the moral panics of the 1980s and 1990s, it became clear that the hype and paranoia had been allowed to do a great deal of damage. Our policy decisions had been heavily influenced by a number of highly publicised sexual abuse trials in day-care centres emanating from the United States. Arguably initiated by the high-profile and (later disproved) accusations against Debbie and Alvin McCuan in 1982 for ritualised sexual abuse of children, anxieties had intensified through a range of court trials, including that of the McMartin preschool worker Raymond Buckey, who in 1983 was accused of involving children in the killing of animals, satanic worship and orgies. Although these charges were also eventually disproved, similar levels of public outrage accompanied the homophobically linked, and eventually overturned, 1984 conviction of the Pittsfield day-care worker Bernard Baran on charges of three counts of child rape and five counts of indecent assault and battery; the 1991 (disproved) accusations against Dale Akiki, who was charged with satanic ritual abuse of children in California; the 1992 (disproved) Martensville satanic child sex scandal; the 1994–95 Wenatchee child abuse prosecutions; and the 1994 (disproved) sexual abuse trials that accompanied the destruction and looting of the Escola Base day-care centre in São Paulo.

But in New Zealand a distinctive educational climate had been shaped by these stories. Here, men, fearing vulnerability to spurious accusations of inappropriate touching, began increasingly avoiding teaching as a career.[39] Concurrently, nurturing physical relationships in schools became ideologically hamstrung. Nicola Power notes that at the time, teachers reported wet and naked children wandering out of pool changing rooms looking for help in getting dressed, and girls lying prone on sportsfields while male teachers sent children to find a female teacher to help.

In 2003, after Alison Jones's research showed that primary school teachers and principals had become reluctant to touch children because of widespread social anxiety about sexual abuse, the NZEI began revising its advice. Its new guidelines, while cautioning against inappropriate behaviour, encouraged 'positive and affirming' contact with students to give emotional support or praise. They emphasised that physical contact was valuable 'when carried out in a professional and responsible manner that is age appropriate'. They recognised that it was acceptable for teachers to hug students, to give pats on the shoulder and to have physical contact when providing medical or toileting assistance.

But an unreasonably high level of anxiety still permeates teaching. While safety from abuse is always important, so too is the need to grow environments that engender trust and positive expression. Research shows us that through childhood, adolescence and adulthood, touch is the primary way that we experience the world around us. We know that when deprived of such intimacy during childhood and adolescence, the deficit can be correlated to heightened levels of adult physical violence.[40]

On a more ubiquitous level, the US psychologist Raymond Lloyd Richmond reminds us that

> *In order to develop emotional intimacy, children need to be touched and caressed. A lack of physical affection and emotional intimacy can cause great psychological pain to a child. Lacking touch and emotional spontaneity in their families, they don't even know how to recognize their own emotional experiences. They repress their emotions, they suffer psychosomatic illnesses, they become socially insecure, and they confuse a need for simple physical affection with sexual desire.*

Perhaps because of such observations, in 2006 the NZEI Physical Code of Conduct was revised. The updated guidelines stated that teachers should assist children in an accident or medical emergency and that physical contact was acceptable when required for effective lesson delivery. These guidelines also made it acceptable for teachers to provide emotional support by comforting children. Despite these changes, teachers remained concerned about the potential for misinterpretation should they adopt a more relaxed attitude to physical contact between themselves and children.

But affection is a healthy part of growing as a human being. It affirms, supports and makes safer those realms of the unknown that we all encounter. It is normal for people to seek out and accept affection. The more we experience it, the greater our depth of understanding of what positive caring is (and, by extension, what it is not).

When we deal with transformative learning, affection and intimacy may take physical or spoken form. Trust is indicative of both, and it is this trust in the intimate that allows us to move learning into very deep levels. I came to understand this in my first year of teaching, despite the fact that it cost me my certification.

the dead cat

Sharlene Hohepa had very thick glasses. She lived just across the road from Tutoi Primary and kept an eye on the school. At seven years of age she was the most effective custodian the place ever had. At any time, day or night, when you pulled into the carpark she would be there. If you reached for the door handle, her face would appear at the window, grinning.

She became my friend. On Sunday afternoons when I went down to school, she would be waiting. She'd help me carry my books into the room and while I worked, preparing the next week's lessons, she would sit over on the sofa, drawing pictures or doing her printing exercises. In my first year of teaching she became a kind of anchor in my life.

Probably the thing that I remember most distinctly about Sharlene was that she had a cat. Well, she didn't really *have* the cat, but because it also frequented the carpark they became associated in people's minds and the two of them developed a mutual kind of respect for each other. The cat was one of those wire-tailed strays that somebody had dumped up the back road, and though no one owned it, it became part of Sharlene's life and, as a result, part of the school.

In the months the cat was with us it developed a routine that ran like clockwork. During morning talks it would wander into the class and nestle between the kids on the sofa. Then, when it came time for printing, it would climb off and meander artfully under their desks. It would pause just long enough for a stroke or a pat and then it would move on again. When the bell rang it could be found out on the seats, hitting up the more naïve students for cheese and tuna sandwiches (and once, a piece of Nicholas Bradstreet's birthday cake.) Then when afternoon school started it would stagger over to the bike racks to sleep off the results of its excess.

It didn't have a name. Like many of those things that become familiar in our lives, it just seemed to be there. It blended in as part of the fabric. The children just called it 'the cat'.

It was on the morning of my visit from the district inspector that Sharlene showed up with it, crying. Sometime during the night the cat had been run over in the carpark and some of the standard four boys, finding it dead, had thrown stones at it and then pushed it under the bus shed. Sharlene had retrieved it, bundled it up in her raincoat and carried it into the classroom. I hugged her for a little while, then we placed the cat on a pillow from the library and she put it on her chair. It seemed very small.

When the class came in for morning talks, word had already reached them and they were obviously distressed. We talked about what it feels like when something you love dies. Lydia told us about her pet calf who got scours, and Ngaire talked about her Nana's tangi, and all the time the cat lay there on Sharlene's seat. We decided in the end that the best thing to do was to bury it, and while Nicholas wanted it dug in down by the war memorial, most people decided that it would be a good idea to make a grave for it at school.

So we wrote stories about the happy times the cat had brought us, drew pictures about it stealing lunches, and I told them the story of the Selfish Giant. During the telling we all sat out on the playing field and made a great daisy chain, and we all cried. It is a very sad story. The cat was out there with us, still on the cushion. When it came time for lunch, we put it in an apple box with flowers and cards and buried it behind the incinerator. Then we washed our hands and sat down to eat together. It seemed strange having lunch without the cat.

The inspector, who had arrived sometime during Lydia's telling of her calf's death from scours, was horrified. He followed the morning like a shadow of disapproval and by afternoon class he decided enough was enough. There had been no spelling and no printing and not a single reading exercise from *The Donkey's Egg*. Instead he'd seen a dead cat and a class full of eight-year-old kids and their teacher crying out on the football field, and he'd seen an incident that should have been discreetly dealt with blown up out of all proportion. At two points during the morning he had suggested that the children would have been better working on their reading programme, and he had serious concerns about the health risks to which they had been subjected.

My probation as a teacher was extended. The next year I was sent to a school in Otara and placed under the watchful eye of an 'experienced' senior teacher. I wasn't aware of it at the time, but the cat and I had broken one of the cardinal rules of education. We had touched the lives and emotions of the children we taught and in so doing we had allowed passion to creep into the system.

the passionate professional

It has always seemed strange to me that we might conceive of an education system that guards against emotion. When I think about it, most of us consider that our greatest lessons have been learnt through their emotional impact. On a social level we've discovered things like 'Some love doesn't last forever', and on an intellectual level 'Water expands when it freezes and that's why my plumbing is wrecked.' We learn these things because we are directly affected by them.

In a climate of curriculum safety it's not hard to understand why students go through adolescence having trouble relating to what is taught. In a media-saturated world that delivers most of its information in emotional packages, people have become used to associating feelings with what they absorb. Whether it is the implications of hegemony or the burial of a dead cat, emotional and sensory stimulation are powerful ways of making links between the world of the learner and the information they absorb.

Although schools operate on a performance-based, production-oriented model, it is the personal relationships inside them that cause education to triumph. We know that people will work well with someone they like. Showing feelings doesn't make us vulnerable as teachers; it makes us complete. It is much easier to attack an emotionless cut-out than it is to attack someone you know. That's why wars reduce enemies to inhuman objects, and that's why if we model ourselves on something inhuman we can expect inhumane responses. It is by being ourselves that we become accessible.

play and display

This accessibility is an important thing. Students need to mix with authentic adults because such people provide natural models of how to navigate flaws, learn productively from failure and resolve problems in effective ways. Kids need to see teachers who trade beyond experience and disobey limited thinking because this is something they are also learning to do. Through childhood and adolescence they navigate the unknown on very visceral levels, and tied inextricably to this is their very strong need to belong. Both of these needs are important, and without careful support they become vulnerable.

While I have always been suspicious of alarmist rhetoric, I don't think many teachers who have been involved in education across a number of generations would deny that the socialising ground of contemporary students has shifted markedly. Today, the peer policing of their behaviour and social 'flaws' is far more explicit, sophisticated and ubiquitous than it was in the past. Most students spend an inordinate amount of time shaping and feeding both an online identity *and* their embodied one. Online environments, while having the potential to expand students' horizons and support networks, also predicate a world of 'play and display'. On social networking sites kids construct and maintain a rigorously edited image of themselves. Here belonging is paramount, all doubt is removed and all flaws hidden (including physical ones). This alternative identity operates under a kind of tyranny of joy, where excitement and engagement become the dominant narrative. Selfies attesting to students' active and unrelentingly positive involvement with life become the dominant reason for taking photographs. These are edited so only the ones that tell the best story of their happiness and beauty are posted. Privacy, introversion and failure have no place in a world which they learn from an early age can be viciously peer policed. This policing of identity is far more rigorous than anything experienced by preceding generations.

Of course social networking is not miasmic; it offers many positive things, but while being an agent for interconnectivity it also has the propensity to disconnect, and is arguably part of a discernible move away from embodied intimacy and authenticity.

An example of this can be illustrated by a relatively overlooked report that surfaced in 2011. Uhls and Greenfield's content analysis study of shifts in dominant values in children's television narratives showed a significant change in the core values being promoted. Its specific findings were sobering. Fame had become the most valued quality in television shows popular with nine- to eleven-year-olds.[41] On a list of 16 values, fame moved from 15th place in both 1987 and 1997 to the most esteemed value in 2007. From 1997 to 2007, kindness and helping others fell from second to thirteenth place. Community feeling (being part of a group), which was ranked the number one value in 1967, 1977 and 1997, and number two in 1987, fell out of the top 10 in 2007. The five highest-ranking values in 2007 (fame, achievement, popularity, image and financial success) replaced the dominant values of a decade earlier (community feeling, benevolence, tradition and self-acceptance).

The study suggested that the biggest change in value profile occurred from 1997 to 2007, when YouTube, Facebook and Twitter exploded in popularity. Yalda Uhls, one of the report's researchers, noted that the findings paralleled existing research in the United States that showed a rise in narcissism and a drop in empathy among college students.

If we remember that a generation earlier most of the children we taught shaped their identities based on local communities, homes and school, then it is useful to remember that our students now strategically groom themselves for hundreds of 'friends' who, on an array of mobile devices, regularly view and comment on their carefully selected selfies and edited life stories. They are on display for these people in a manner beyond anything experienced by earlier generations. Of course, what is on display in this seemingly flawless world is not an authentic self but its hungry imitation. The authentic self walks into our classrooms every day. It is what we deal with in a less edited dynamic where human beings mix with other human beings in embodied ways. The awkwardness, conflicts and tentative triumphs are part of an ordinary dynamic of learning and transformation. This is why authenticity, intimacy and truthfulness in learning and teaching are so important. It is why humanely passionate teachers count.

protests at the gate

Although the need for authenticity and trust is important in helping students shape realistic identities for themselves, the same can
be said for teachers. Like many of my colleagues, much of who I
am as an educator has been shaped by transformative experiences
I have encountered in the classroom. This is not platitudinous
rhetoric: such things occur in very profound ways. When we work
in high-trust environments, both students and teachers are open
to accommodating things outside of their scope of experience. I
would like to give you an example.

I once taught at a school that had been built on a dump. Like
most buildings on the site its woodwork room was braced onto
poles that ran down to a rock substrate well below the surface. At
the back of this workshop stood three old Tanner wood lathes,
and below the first one was a wooden trapdoor. Mostly people
ignored it, except on the odd occasion when an enterprising student felt that sweeping sawdust down the hole might be quicker
than reaching for a shovel and depositing it into the rubbish box.
Over time, because of the land subsidence caused by the settling
of the dump, the space beneath the trapdoor increased. Back in
the early 1980s when the Dawn Raids[42] were still occurring, the
hole twice hid Tongan students when a coded ring on my phone
acted as a warning that immigration officials were at the school
office looking for them. Quickly and quietly the kids were hustled
out of sight. When the officers arrived at the room, the class continued working as normal. One of the students would set a job up
on the wood lathe so that they were standing over the trapdoor.
The officers would make polite inquiries about absences and check
the class roll (which was strategically left unmarked until the end
of a lesson). About 10 minutes after the officers left there would
be another ring on my phone and the hidden students would be

helped back up into the classroom. During the immigration crack-downs these Pacific Island kids were very vulnerable. They would leave home before dawn as a way of ensuring a degree of safety. Nobody talked openly about what certain teachers were doing at this time. We protected them as best we could, even though we knew that we were breaking the law.

But kids and their families do not forget such things. I have learned over time a great deal about the power of remembered trust. A few years after the Dawn Raids subsided the nature of this loyalty came back in a very dramatic way. At this time my partner was dying of Aids. It was a difficult period because while I was trying to care for him we were receiving things like small parcels of faeces and rusty razor blades wrapped in cigarette packets in the mail. This was because at this time I was active in the homosex-ual law reform movement. Often at strange hours in the night we would be woken by abusive phone calls from people who shouted Bible verses down the line then hung up. It is hard protecting somebody so near death from such things.

The school knew about our relationship and my involvement in the law reform movement and they were supportive. They were aware at the time that legally we could have been evicted from our flat, denied goods and services, fired from our jobs and faced up to seven years' imprisonment, all without recourse to legal protec-tion. The students I taught also knew about our relationship. My partner and I had been to a couple of the school balls and they followed his successes as a noted New Zealand athlete. A lot of lesbian and gay parents had begun to send their children to the school because they knew there was a safe environment for them. However, for many of the Pacific Island students things were quite difficult. A number of prominent pastors in their communities at this time advocated strongly against the decriminalisation of gay men, and some of their families had been encouraged to circulate a petition aimed at stopping the reform of laws in New Zealand.

On the morning of 12 April 1985 when I walked into my workshop the room was silent. The night before the police had closed a public meeting where I had been speaking, and on the television news my students had watched me being dragged out. As I laid out tools for the lesson I noticed on the blackboard at the front of the room someone had scrawled the word 'FAG'. I ignored it. I methodically marked the roll and went over the schedule for the period. When we were ready to begin the lesson I told them they could turn on the machines, but nobody moved. The room was silent.

Eventually Semisi put up his hand. It wasn't a question. 'You were on television.'

I looked at them, this class of young men and women with whom I worked so closely. I opened the workshop each Saturday so they could come down to continue with their projects. We ate lunches wrapped in greaseproof paper together and talked enthusiastically about the things they wanted to do with their lives. But today they were frightened.

'Yes, I was speaking about something I believe in.'

Still nobody moved, but they kept glancing furtively out the workshop windows. Finally Taniella spoke up. 'Do you know there are people at the front gate?'

I knew what they were referring to. Apparently some of the meeting organisers had found out where I worked and they were protesting about my being allowed to teach at the school. They had placards and they were parading around the school carpark.

'I know.'

The silence continued. I hadn't wanted this to happen, but I was learning that sometimes the outside world crashes into your classroom. At that point Taniella and two of the other boys shuffled sideways, got up from their workbenches and started walking towards the door. I thought they were leaving the class. When I asked where they were going, one of them picked up a piece of wood. Taniella looked at me and said, 'We're going out there to sort them out.'

Sometimes I misread things. What I had mistaken for anger was in fact loyalty. I realised they were trying to protect me. I hastily explained that I was okay, and I told them that I was exercising my right to speak and we had to protect other people's right to do the same. I told them that's what living in a democracy is about.

The boys stood awkwardly at the door for a moment, then began walking back to their benches. However, halfway back Taniella turned around and walked up to the blackboard. He picked up the duster and went to rub out the word scrawled word across the wall.

I asked him, 'Did you write that?'

When he said 'No', I told him to leave it there.

In that pragmatic way of 15-year-old kids, the lesson settled down and within a few minutes I was helping them to realign dovetail joints and laminate timber. I had expected 'FAG' to stay on the blackboard but by the end of the lesson it had disappeared. I don't know who rubbed it out. What I do know is when it came time to tidy up, the room received an extraordinary cleaning. I didn't have to ask. Machines were wiped down, floors swept within an inch of their lives, and tools were straightened in their racks. They knew how I valued such things. At the end of the lesson I walked them out of the technology block. I was concerned that the protest might have moved into the body of the school and I didn't want them caught up in it. However, I needn't have worried. Apparently very early in the piece the women from the school office had advanced on the protesters with the grace of Doberman Pinschers and the picket had dissipated.

I think I was probably shaking a little when I returned to the workshop. The room was empty and quiet. I picked up my roll book and turned to walk into my office. That was when I saw it. On the corner of my bench was a pile of sandwiches wrapped up in greaseproof paper. Beside it on a torn piece of paper was a rapidly scrawled note. It said, 'For your lunch Welby'.

It was the nature of loyalty.

By the end of the day the story of the protest had taken on legendary proportions. The kids kept popping over to the workshop to check if I was okay, and when I did my routine lunchtime duty it all felt like a re-run scene from a Ghandi movie. But this wasn't heroic. It was simply the nature of love. It is what happens when people trust other people, when they work together in worlds without road maps and where humanity and passion are a normal and committed part of learning together.

Such things are transformative.

* * *

PART FIVE

THE BUSINESS OF SUCCESS

It might be useful now to look at the relationship between disobedience and success. We know that creativity is based on thinking beyond compliance, and that productive disobedience can cause us to experience the world in more passionate and expansive ways. Given these insights, we might ask how people use these things to change environments in which they operate. Perhaps as a start we should look at why schools are structured the way they are.

the roots of hierarchy

Most of us grew up in an education system whose roots ran deeply into hierarchical models of power and management. Schools, like many institutions developed during the eighteenth and nineteenth centuries (including hospitals, police, prisons, asylums, factories and orphanages), tend to have a common structure. Traditionally you can move between them and find similar concepts of hierarchy, pyramid control, promotion and tiered accountability. Their design assumes that power and privilege are gained and that change is normally initiated from the top.

Such hierarchies are a remnant of an antiquated structure that may be attributed in part to the Industrial Revolution. Departments, chancellors, vice-chancellors, principals, deputy principals, professors, associate professors, senior lecturers, junior lecturers and ordinary classroom teachers mirror a system that divides students into juniors, seniors, class leaders and prefects (or their equivalent). These divisions indicate what is made available or expected (and when), and they determine incremental progression and levels of privilege.

These hierarchies are identifiable in the physical design of most traditional schools in New Zealand, with the principal's office positioned at the front of the institution (normally close to the site of public reception) and tiers of influence arranged in decreasing order of status as you move towards the back of the establishment. Although such spatial structures may be slowly dissolving, the hierarchical management of education remains deeply embedded, along with the constructions of power and reward that govern it.

the ideological makeover

Since 1877 this structure has formed the substrate from which mass schooling in New Zealand has been built. However, although the model has been formative in how we experience education, it has undergone significant ideological shifts. One of the most pronounced of these occurred during the late 1980s and early 1990s. At this time New Zealand stepped into the limelight as the first country in the world to account for its finances as a business (rather than a nation). The government considered the state as a balance sheet. According to Charles Handy, this approach revealed that 'its assets, state companies, roads, lands and buildings, financial reserves and investments totalled NZ$14.4 billion less than its liabilities, by which it meant its borrowing and its pension scheme'.[43] Under this new business model, New Zealand was found to be economically unsustainable. Among the costly issues was an ageing population and no sense of where the money would be sourced from to pay pensions and superannuation. The country was also managing the highest number of students in tertiary education in its history, with no way to afford the cost.

So, in the late 1980s the Labour government introduced a new economic system based on the vision of the minister of finance, Roger Douglas. Under this system New Zealand became part of a global economy. Tariffs and trade protection were all but eliminated. Government departments and state-owned enterprises were sold off and privatised. Hospitals and educational institutions ceased to be public services and were expected to function like any other business.

The changes rolled out over one tempestuous decade. The ideological shift was controversial and in retrospect viewed by many as problematic. Jane Kelsey noted that between 1989 and 1992 the number of New Zealanders estimated to be living in poverty grew by at least 35 per cent;[44] Danuta Wasserman and colleagues recorded a youth suicide rate that increased to one of the highest in the developed world;[45] and Stuart Bramhall observed that health care experienced a significant deterioration in standards among working- and middle-class people.[46] In addition, many of the promised economic benefits of the experiment failed to materialise. Between 1986 and 1993 the unemployment rate rose from 3.6 to 11 per cent. Between 1985 and 1992 OECD economies grew by an average of 20 per cent while New Zealand's economy shrank by 1 per cent over the same period. From 1984 to 1993 inflation averaged 9 per cent per year, New Zealand's credit rating dropped twice and foreign debt quadrupled.[47]

In this new national order, organisations were seen as businesses and people became resources. All of this was accompanied by a new rhetoric. Downsizing, privatising, restructuring, performance indicators and human capital became part of a new vernacular. In this brave new world we were expected to work 'smarter', meet targets, and achieve outcomes. 'Lean and mean' became an aspiration rather than a criticism. We became 'human resources' that were managed by groups bearing the same name. At worst, we were reduced to labour units. In tertiary education, learners were now called EFTS[48] and education providers accorded value to their programmes based on how fully they were EFTS-populated.

As employees, when we were no longer useful we were 'redundant' to the needs of the organisation. The new euphemisms of corporate irresponsibility became as sweet as saccharine. Unnecessary workers were 'released to their futures' (fired), 'let go safely' (fired), 'given the opportunity to start their new job search' (fired), 'redirected' (fired) or 'given premature retirement' (fired). In this new climate, where people lost their jobs through restructuring or remained in employment but saw their colleagues disappear, workers began to lose faith in organisations as a trusted component of their personal future. Elkin, Jackson and Inkson, in discussing this phenomenon, note that what surfaced was 'an increasing emphasis on the individual rather than the organisation as the key unit of economic life'.[49]

As we became disenfranchised we were expected to become more competitive. We became part of evidence-based, outcome-oriented teams, where, paradoxically, each of us needed to report individual success, and we met regularly with line managers to tick off performance reviews that itemised what we had achieved.

In this ideological reshaping, schools became increasingly competitive, both internally and in their wider communities. Progressively, league tables and articles on comparative performance became the subject of closely read magazine and newspaper articles. Teachers were expected to become performers and were measured to ensure they met the requirements of efficiency and accountability. In this dynamic, assessment became a tool for measuring student and teacher success at the same time. The organisations in which we worked were judged on their effectiveness in turning inputs into outputs. Schools became 'education providers' who were expected to compete for clients. Communities became our customers and our effectiveness was increasingly compared.

During this period tertiary education in New Zealand also became reconfigured along market lines, with an increasing emphasis placed on student choice, provider competition, performance indicators, accountability mechanisms and corporate models of governance and ownership.[50] The emphasis moved university and polytechnic education increasingly towards measured performance. Indicative of this was the Tertiary Education Commission's introduction, two years after its establishment, of a Performance-Based Research Fund (PBRF), which financially rewards research based on ranked lists of outputs. Despite writers like Curtis and Matthewman criticising the initiative for demoting research to a form of revenue generation,[51] within months the strategic compilation of research portfolios became the ubiquitous concern of the nation's academic staff and their managers.

impediments and expectations

However, embedded within this increasing emphasis on measurable, rewardable performance was an inherent disability. At a time when there was much discussion about the need to develop organisations that could embrace change and flexibility, education's preoccupation with addressing indicators began to impede its ability to deal with potential. This is because, as teachers and their organisations were rewarded for meeting performance review indicators, there was little incentive to creatively engage with instability. The anxious pursuit of measurable productivity ankle-strapped the flexibility required for high levels of innovation.

And then something unusual came flooding across the doorstep: a new and distinctively different generation of employee. The millennials who began entering the profession at this time had no conscious memory of learning to use a computer. Their experience of education (both formal and informal) had evolved in an environment where there was unprecedented access to intellectual, technical and emotional support. Much of this had operated beyond the approval and permission of a singular authority figure. As kids they had grown up online, in non-hierarchical social networks that operated on levels of approval and choice rather than earned status. Their experience of history had witnessed ordinary people mobilising and posting information beyond the constraints imposed by governing bodies. Economically they had learned to consume goods that used everything from open-source software to online auction sites like Trade Me. These systems had allowed alternative economies to operate for them without the prior approval or control of single, power-centred authorities like finance companies, marketing firms or distributors. This was all normalised. Such expectations and experiences were hardwired into their identities.

Tamara Erickson has noted that these new workers, administrators and managers brought with them higher expectations of immediacy, involvement and acknowledgement, coupled with an understanding that systems function with multiple opportunities and truths.[52] Their advanced levels of intrinsic technological understanding and exposure to alternative power traditions made them part of a more questioning population that expected more flexibility, respect and personal engagement in organisations.

And herein lies a problem. As educational institutions pursue talent, few innovators are attracted to professional structures that expect them to be a cog in a machine. Highly innovative people may train as teachers, but they rarely stay long in the system, or if they do they seek out organisations that offer them higher levels of autonomy and acknowledgement. Exposure to new forms of organisational effectiveness, greater levels of experienced empowerment and the speed of information access have all radically changed the way people measure value in a potential workplace. Wounded hierarchies that doggedly insist on treating power as a limited and privileged resource increasingly find themselves unable to attract or hold on to highly innovative educators. They are also less able to grow the generations of thinkers whose worlds and values differ profoundly from their own. Such organisations are unable to adapt core structures and values, so they are not flexible enough to operate at the vanguard of opportunity. They cannot naturally grow risk-taking leaders. Instead, what they reward are people who can minimalise disruption, read agendas, mouth the rhetoric of change, strategise time and resources and, most importantly, report strategically on their successes.

In such environments innovative thinkers either pack up and leave[53] or become someone they are not. If they remain in limiting environments, they commit to an agenda that is increasingly removed from the unstable and idiosyncratic wonder of learning. They perform a constrained, reportable professionalism, and somewhere, deep down inside, they look at what they are doing and they know that it isn't right.

care bears with claws

In 1982 the toy company Kenner released a strange species of animal. Their debut was touted as 'the biggest character launch in the history of retailing'.[54] You may remember them as plush, brightly coloured toys, each with a specialised insignia on its stomach. They were called Care Bears, and they had their own television series, movies, publications, music videos, toy lines and, significantly, a string of school supplies. Commercially they were hugely successful. Their blissful natures flooded schools like candy-coloured molasses. But I always felt uneasy about them. Perhaps it was because they made goodness so simple. Care Bears were unrelentingly nice. Their beatific presence graced classroom walls, school sick bays and reception offices. They lived in a world where good was sweet and bad was nasty and there were clear divisions between the two.

But care is a multifaceted thing. This is because, as human beings, we are flawed. You and I and all of the people we work with. Whether we see ourselves as leaders or managers or followers, adored or vilified, we are all forced to work with our flaws and the flaws of those around us. This takes complex care.

Care is a difficult thing to grow when you work in a competitive environment that relies on people being recognised and having individual success attributed to them. Back in 1936 Dale Carnegie misquoted the American educational reformer John

Dewey in stating, 'The deepest urge in human nature is the desire to be important.'[55] His statement has littered self-help manuals and books on management ever since, perhaps because there is a seed of truth in it. It may sound a little uncharitable, but we all pursue our own importance. We may like to frame ourselves as altruistic, caring and morally refined, but we're not. Not a single one of us is a pastel-coloured Care Bear.

The deep urge to be valued drives both our finest and our most abject behaviours. It has caused artists to create wonders, sports people to push the limits of human capacity, business leaders to build empires and philanthropists to require that their names be fixed with bronze plaques onto the walls of the institutions they fund. The desire to be valued is the source of our need to be identified and respected. Today, it is the reason why marginalised people squander their most intimate relationships and reputations for a moment of recognition on tabloid talk shows, why selfies clog social media sites, and why people spend inordinate amounts of money and time to become legendary heroes in virtual worlds.

competition and resentment

In institutions based on competitive models of advancement and recognition, the desire for importance is used to generate commitment. Such systems are predicated on a belief that the triumph of the individual is a rigorous and inherently laudable phenomenon. If we don't triumph or are the victim of another person's success, we are taught that the fault is our own. We are seen as weak or complaining, or lacking in the robust camaraderie required to survive in a hard-playing team. This is why issues such as professional bullying took generations to surface as a serious concern in bureaucratic organisations. People had learned to blame themselves for being a victim and to feel disempowered in standing up to a structure where the ability to manipulate and assert authority was seen as a quality.

But competitive, hierarchical organisations also grow something else, and it is something we are often reluctant to talk about openly. It is professional jealousy. Professional jealousy lies at the base of many of the interpersonal conflicts we encounter and it can take many forms. It occurs in the resentment generated by the jostle for discipline status in schools, or the allocation of budgets, grants or promotion. On a more personal level it arises when we resent lazy colleagues who self-promote to positive effect or graft our efforts onto their personal profiles of success. At its most damaging, however, professional jealousy causes people in hierarchical systems to protect their position. In doing this they can impede others who they feel may threaten their station or expose limitations in their level of competence. This becomes particularly evident when talented people begin demonstrating skills and usefulness that someone higher up the ladder doesn't possess. Such displays of ability can be seen as dangerous. As a result, the threatened individual may bully, disparage or undermine. This sounds awful, but few people who have worked in a hierarchical system can claim not to have encountered such things. Popularity, effectiveness, initiative and talent are very threatening to people who hold hierarchical positions through ambition rather than talent. So is disobedience.

Logically, the first people to leave under the constraints of such management are the passionately driven innovators. As they exit, the organisations they populated stagnate.

the heroic manager

Stagnant institutions often contain a certain kind of manager, whom we might describe as heroic. Traditionally the heroic manager is a singular creature. Their self-image of a confident, visionary problem solver has been shaped since childhood. From the edited personas of historical world leaders to the celebrity posters that decorated their bedroom walls, their role models were fashioned as individual and heroic. When they grew up and entered the workforce, the idea of the powerful, individualistic business leader, political change agent and representative of nationhood continued to be simplified to a heroic ideal. Stripped of the realities of their support systems, these leaders were presented as all-knowing task assigners, who monitored and managed using a dynamic of command, control and coercion. At their most euphoric they were seen as charismatic individuals who made independent decisions and were credited with being the primary driver of their organisation's success. Of course this isn't true, but with our need to conceive of ourselves as potentially important and valued, such simplistic concepts of leadership can be very palatable.

Heroic managers can sometimes be relatively efficient, but rarely are they effective leaders. This is because no single person in an organisation – no matter how talented, well resourced or powerful – can compare to a dedicated group of committed people pooling expertise, experience and recognition in the pursuit of common goals. It's quite obvious really. The applied talents of one person are, of course, less than the collective talents of many. But heroic systems generally fail to understand this. In the end they become self-defeating because the more heroic they are, the more they increase the gap between dependency and empowerment.

the stolen handbag

Perhaps I can illustrate this with the story of a heroic manager and two disobedient teachers. In the late 1970s I was teaching in a primary school that served a community with a very high crime rate. A lot of the kids came from gang families. At this school vandalism had become so commonplace that we had been instructed to have our vehicles out of the carpark by 3.30pm because the school would not take responsibility for any damage. On Monday mornings we would often arrive to find at least one classroom trashed. I can't say that it was a very happy place to work, either for the students or for the teachers.

But in this school I once observed something extraordinary. It concerned two first-year teachers who were managed by a junior school principal. This principal ran a tight ship. In heroic fashion she assigned tasks and ensured that her instructions were fulfilled. She checked the teachers' rolls, their marking and their evaluation sheets. She praised them when they did well and reprimanded them when they disobeyed. I use the word 'disobeyed' because the term formed a major part of her lexicon. Essentially, to disobey was to question one of her decisions. As a principal she set clear rules and people were expected to follow them. She knew how the system worked and how to keep order. There was never any trouble in her classes. You could walk past the windows of Room 4 and hear the purr of obedience. She could solve problems, set strategies and make decisions. She was as heroic as she was observant, and she held the second-highest position in the school.

One afternoon near the end of our first term the principal arrived back in her classroom from lunch duty to find that her handbag was missing. After making enquiries it became evident that the same thing had happened to the two young teachers who shared the block with her. It was immediately clear that this had been a deliberate theft and she intended to get to the bottom of it. After lunch she lined her class up at the back of her room and one by one questioned them about the incident. She told them when they looked into her eyes that she could see if they were lying. She instructed the two teachers in her charge to do the same thing with their classes.

After discovering to her consternation that either there were no thieves in her class or it housed a number of eight-year-old fabricators who had the audacity to tell her a bare-faced lie, the principal visited the other teachers. They assured her that their children knew nothing about the theft, but when she questioned the students she quickly discovered that the teachers had disobeyed her instructions and not lined them up for an eye-to-eye interrogation. She was outraged. She told the young women that they had not followed a professional instruction. She explained that in teaching you have to learn to work as a team and she would not be undermined.

By the end of the day, when the school bell rang, still nobody had owned up. The handbags had contained car keys and driver's licences, so all three teachers were forced to get a lift home with a colleague.

The next morning when we arrived for the 8.30am staff meeting we found a police officer waiting at the office. He had been invited to talk to us about security. During the meeting we sat politely and listened to his advice, then the junior principal thanked him for his address and informed us that he would be visiting each of our classes in turn to talk with the children. Perplexed, we glanced at each other. This hadn't been discussed and I could see that the two first-year teachers were looking especially worried. This was the time of the Dawn Raids in South Auckland and tensions between the police and the families of many of our children were running very high. Eventually one of the young teachers raised her hand and suggested politely that perhaps we might delay things until another time.

The temperature in the staffroom dropped 5 degrees. We all felt it. The junior school principal had set the activity and here in front of a representative of the New Zealand police force her authority had been challenged. Her smile was like titanium. She carefully stated the times the officer would be at our classes and explained that she would personally be there to introduce him.

When we left the staffroom the door was locked behind us. This was a morning ritual because it was believed that the children at the school couldn't be trusted not to steal the biscuits from the fridge. I remember walking across the asphalt with the two teachers as they discussed how they were going to handle the situation. They knew these kids. Their refusal to line them up and question them the day before wasn't going to help when the district inspector came around to assess their teaching progress. The junior school principal had been quite clear about it. She expected obedience.

In the end things played out as she had arranged. The officer spoke to each of the classes. The kids sat there wide-eyed and frightened, and in one, Manu Tu'ifua started crying and asked why the policeman had taken his brother away. In consternation the officer explained that he hadn't, but it was no good. The kids all thought they were going to jail for stealing the principal's handbag. To help retrieve the situation the officer took the class outside to see his bright new police car and he offered to give them a ride in it. There were no takers.

The week limped from bad to worse. The principal instituted lunchtime class detentions and enticements for the kids to 'privately' share anything they knew with her. Nobody did. Although the two first-year teachers were instructed to follow her lead, they continued to minimalise their involvement. Instead they tried to work out another way of approaching the problem. Fortuitously, on Friday mornings the principal went out to do advisory work in another school. So putting aside printing and spelling exercises, the two teachers joined their classes in one room and showed the kids how to make paper hats. They were fashioned from newsprint and in 10 minutes each child had two of them on their table.

Then the teachers sat down and talked with the kids about the favourite thing they owned. The variety was broad, from a Great Uncle Bulgaria Womble to a pair of dancing shoes received from a grandmother, from a pit bull terrier called Fooh Fooh, to a greenstone necklace. The children drew this thing on one of their hats and wrote a sentence about why they loved it.

Then the teachers did something strange. They asked all of the children to put their hat on the table and dash outside for the fastest run they could make around the perimeter of the playground. When they returned five minutes later all of their hats were missing. The women said that someone had taken them. While the kids looked taken aback, the teachers asked them what it would feel like if the thing they loved the most was really stolen. Once everybody had spoken, the teachers briefly talked about something they had liked in their handbag and how they felt when it was gone.

Then the teachers led the kids into the room that had been left empty when the classes had joined together. Laid out on a table was a set of hats. But these had nothing on them. No drawings. Just blank. When the children went to pick them up they realised that the second hat they had made had been cleverly stapled over the one onto which they had drawn. The trouble was that now nobody knew which hat belonged to whom. But they were asked not to look and to simply put on a hat they liked. When everyone was suitably attired they were led back to the other room.

Although this may have seemed a bit odd, the teachers sat them down and talked with them. The kids knew they were probably wearing a hat that wasn't theirs, and that hat had on it something that was the most important thing in the world to someone else in the class. The teachers encouraged them to talk about how it would feel to be caught with the stolen hat. Then they discussed ways that you could return what was valuable to another person without being thought of as a thief.

The kids thought very hard about this. The answers ranged from direct honesty and an apology, to sending the hat in the mail, to handing it in to the police station, or giving it to a friend to return, or leaving it somewhere conspicuous. To be honest, a couple of boys also suggested just burning the evidence. But what was interesting was the way the teachers helped the kids *feel* what it was like to have something taken, and then to *feel* what it was like to be potentially blamed. Then they worked with the group to help find solutions to a problem nobody knew how to answer: how do you safely return something you have stolen?

I know that stories like this are supposed to have magnificent endings, but this is not a perfect world. There were no profound examples of a child standing up in the class, confessing their mistake and offering a heartfelt apology. But on the following Monday one of the young teachers found her room broken into. Nothing had been trashed and nothing was missing, but in one of the cupboards were three handbags. Yes, the cash was missing, the chewing gum had gone and so apparently had a packet of antacids that may have been mistaken for lollies, but the keys and the driver's licences were there. There were also some other things, belonging to heaven knows who, apportioned through the bags: somebody's lipstick, a used case of eyeliner and a half-empty packet of Pall Mall cigarettes. These were carefully divided between the two young women's handbags. The principal's was returned without embellishment.

The two teachers in this incident had been disobedient. They were given clear instructions on how to deal with the problem and they were made aware that there was going to be a price for their lack of compliance. But between them they had formed an effective solution. They told me that the idea of the double hats had surfaced from a difficult conversation at the end of the day when they were waiting for a lift home. Had they been asked for their ideas at the outset, perhaps the outcome might have been arrived at faster.

This was back in the 1970s and I have no idea where these women are now, but I am sure that in some capacity they are leading people. Their propensity to disobey what they sensed was wrong and to construct creative alternatives, even when they were apparently disempowered, says something about their strength and character. Their leadership through the situation was complex and nuanced. They went beyond heroic solution-making. What they demonstrated was raw leadership: creativity, co-creation, collaboration and productive disobedience.

These are the things that we would aspire to in excellent teaching. However, these skills were to become increasingly difficult to exercise in the years that followed. The spirit of New Zealand schooling was about to undergo a significant shift.

new organisational leaders

In the 1980s, at the time our education system was experiencing its business-led reforms like Administering for Excellence and Tomorrow's Schools, the largely unquestioned model of leadership being rewarded was heroic. Effective teachers and principals were conceived of as individuals, and decisions were increasingly made at a national level by similar people who did little to consult with those working at the chalk face. Heroic experts were seen as having greater insight into how education should be reformed.[56] Such people drove change, fixed problems and were appointed for their individual expertise.

However, in the same period that all of this heroically fashioned reform was being rolled out, management writers such as James Eicher had begun to identify new, antithetical models of organisational leadership that were enabling companies such as Ortho Biotech and Levi Strauss & Co to suddenly burst ahead of their competitors. These companies had recently undergone deep ideological and structural changes based on flexibility and inclusion. In them, power had become disseminated and an emphasis was placed on shared practices enacted by people at all levels of the organisation. Collaboration ('we') and shared commitment and responsibility in these companies had replaced the triumphant 'I'.

Yet these new models of organisational leadership were not euphoric fairy tales. In the hard world of commercial enterprise they had become extremely successful. In these businesses, positional leaders still existed but they were a very different kind of creature. They could develop and support a broad network of colleagues practising personal leadership who took responsibility for and ownership of what was going on. They encouraged risk-taking and people speaking up and changing what needed to be changed based on their intimate knowledge of a situation and the culture surrounding it. In their companies talented people got the support they needed, but they were also held accountable for acting on their personal leadership. The phenomenon was called 'post-heroic' leadership.

the demise of the manager

What these businesses were recognising and growing was shared leadership and potential. This was very different to their competitors, who had traditionally groomed and promoted managers into so-called positions of leadership while running off actual leaders. Before global economies, digitalised worlds and plural knowledges, the well-managed, hierarchical model could operate as a substitute for leadership. In fact, such organisations could be almost leaderless, run on the efforts of middle managers. The companies were only required to tick over and workers were simply meant to be obedient. However, by 1994 middle managers were increasingly being identified as an encumbrance. Commentators such as John Huey and Ricardo Sookdeo observed that highly effective corporations were increasingly flattening their structures and distributing traditional management tasks across a wider range of workers. But as this began happening, these organisations also became aware that they had within their workforces an alarming paucity of real leaders. There weren't enough men and women who people genuinely respected and trusted, who were able to build high levels of empowerment without the needy ego that was central to the heroic model. Because hierarchical models had not been able to attract or reward such talents, these potential leaders were working elsewhere.

competing models

In education today you can find post-heroic leaders, but they tend to gravitate towards organisations that give them room to move. They do not function well in a leader/follower system, but thrive in environments where influence can flow in two directions. Such leaders are normally significant reformers because they learn from, listen to and are 'led' by others. People normally like working with them. I work as a consultant to a number of large organisations where both heroic and post-heroic leaders operate, and I'd like to compare a couple of examples. Although unique, their generic profiles are probably familiar to you.

The first is a woman working in a university, who has become very influential. She is genuinely interested in learning from others, no matter who they are or what their job is. She greets the guy blowing the leaves off the footpath and the CEO in the same way. She recognises that she is neither omniscient nor without flaws, so she is quite happy admitting when she is wrong. One of the significant features of her leadership is the way that she builds collective experiences and systems. She also rewards and celebrates innovation and commitment. However, these celebrations are a consequence of staff nominations, not her own. She is popular because she is both transparent and approachable. When you pop into her office, her desk is tucked up against a wall and she sits at a table in the middle of the room with you. She is a very good listener, discerning quickly between what is evidence and thinking and what is just table-banging and self-promotion. She has learned to work with more than one variable, more than one group of people, more than one truth and more than one conflicting demand. Interestingly, she does not call herself a leader.

But other people do.

Conversely, in another organisation, I know a hardworking man who sees himself as a heroic leader. He is well intentioned and he tries to do an effective job. He likes to be admired and he is very good at publicly fronting the effective initiatives that he manages. He proudly talks about *his* team and *his* department, but you rarely hear him use one of their names when he is telling stories of success. He is ambitious, strategic and an excellent networker. He appears to care, but he quickly reads 'who's who' and responds to those in power while placating others. He consults his team, but often this is after a decision has already been made (covertly) higher up. He also sees himself as the final decision-maker and he gets very hurt if he feels his authority has been circumvented. He uses the rhetoric of leadership elegantly, but he rarely appears when it's time to do the donkeywork. Instead, he tries to inject motivation into people by being an inspiring individual. He allocates tasks and people comply, but information does not flow freely among those with whom he works. Much of his management happens behind closed doors because he has learned that in a hierarchical system you need to protect knowledge and decision-making because they are your claim to distinction.

People in the organisation feel sorry for him because he tries very hard yet he feels betrayed by the system. He finds it difficult to understand why his employees don't trust him even though they are nice to his face. In truth, because of his need to be seen as a heroic leader he fails to gain much respect. He is unhappy because innovation and productive change, although espoused, do not appear to happen. He feels unappreciated by his team and disabled by the hierarchy above him. He complains a lot because despite his networking and deferral to those he sees as above him, he effects very little change.

Perhaps, though, he may be comforted to know that he is not alone. David Bradford and Allan Cohen have estimated that 90 per cent of managers in business operate from a heroic leadership mindset. That is, they assume sole responsibility for setting their organisation's objectives, co-ordinating subordinates, and monitoring and managing their performances. In education such managers – be they teachers, team leaders, principals, deans or individuals – have bought into an idea of individual heroism, and despite having learned a new rhetoric of collaboration, they end up practising only its imitation. Around them, increasingly, post-heroic leadership empowers and draws on a greater mass of talent. By comparison, the individual hero manages what is, at best, obedient efficiency.

But we need to be realistic here. Post-heroic leadership is a refined skill and not everybody possesses it. We know that such people are a limited resource. Often their talent is not linked to ambition, so they are not automatically found among senior managers who are already successfully operating in competitive systems. In fact it is quite common to find such leaders functioning parallel to, or outside of, hierarchies. This is partly because much of their ability is predicated on a diminished ego and the propensity to genuinely empower and acknowledge other people's contributions. As generally popular leaders they are able to work with others to create and gain commitment to tangible visions. To achieve this, they authentically decentralise themselves (somewhat in the manner of a good coach), and they build shared responsibility based on mutual influence and an expectation of shared decision-making.

five features of post-heroic leadership

So how might we recognise a post-heroic leader? Well, I am loath to have this sound like a chapter crimped out of a self-help book, but such people often display similar, distinctive characteristics, both personally and in the way they lead organisations. Five of these characteristics are worth examining.

Growing other people

First, you will often see such leaders investing in initiatives that develop personal leadership at all levels of their organisation (from students to teachers to ground staff to administrators and executives). So, beyond the rhetoric of inclusiveness, they strategically empower the people they work with. They ask others what they need, they take leadership potential seriously, and they invest in talent potentially greater than their own.

Creating high-trust environments

Second, post-heroic leaders place a great deal of emphasis on decentralised, high-trust environments. This means they do not micro-manage. Instead, they mix responsibility with personal humility. They trust the working parties they co-create with their colleagues, which means they do not demand incessant reporting. They grow leadership but also expect very high levels of personal responsibility. What is significant is that they do not unrelentingly position themselves in the seat of final approval. Although responsible for their organisation and attentive to its development, they trust other leaders to make good decisions.

This is not an easy thing to do. It requires genuinely believing in other people as much as you believe in yourself, and not all people can do this. This is why it is imitations of empowerment that are so commonly experienced in organisations. In the illusory models, teams are normally not co-created but assigned, and decision-making is generally cosmetic, limited and destined for final approval.

You may be very familiar with models such as these, but let me give you an example you will probably recognise from your past. Back in the early 1970s when I was at college there surfaced a flurry of revolutionary writing about education. I am not sure why it happened, but over a decade and a half New Zealanders were reading a plethora of deeply questioning books about how we learn and the power structures that govern how educational institutions run. Although publications like *The Little Red School Book* were banned at our college, those of us who hid it under the curling sandwiches in the bottom of our school bags clung to the intensity of its questioning. Because of books like this, a number of students, along with their teachers, began enquiring into A.S. Neill's Summerhill School experiment and reading books like Ivan Illich's *Deschooling Society*, Neil Postman and Charles Weingartner's *Teaching as a Subversive Activity* and John Holt's *How Children Fail*. To a generation raised on the expectation that schools knew what they were doing, such writing prompted a serious wake-up call.

In response to the questions these books raised, our college, like many schools across the country, set up a student council. Magnanimously it was explained that we would all now be part of the decision-making process, and that our involvement in how our college ran was an honour and should be treated with respect and maturity. It sounded great. This was a brave new world. Those of us populating the outer rings of influence stubbed out our cigarettes, tucked in our shirts and began to pay close attention.

In the optimistic rush that accompanied a promise of inclusiveness the students who had been hand-picked by the senior teachers offered a raft of proposals. They suggested that all compulsory, extra-curricular activities should be made voluntary (this included the annual cross-country race and the compulsory school speech contest). They wanted a wider choice of school uniform options so that poorer families were not forced into buying monogrammed clothing from an exclusive provider that overpriced its garments, and they wanted to establish an independent student radio station free from vetted playlists and edited commentary.

What happened? Well, you know what happened. The school management found themselves mauled by a gummy lamb so they graciously thanked the students and explained that the issues were more complex than they realised. As a result, nothing was implemented. The student council had been a token initiative designed to look contemporary. At best it was consultative, but it was never intended to be co-creative. The councillors got to wear badges on their blazers and they were clustered together for a photograph in the school magazine, but in the end all they got to do was choose the theme for the annual school ball and dress the hall accordingly. By the close of the year the whole thing had become a playground joke. Eventually, based on accusations of student apathy, the staff disbanded the initiative.

What damaged this initiative was, of course, related to trust. When we don't trust people we resort to consultation instead of empowerment. Consulting safely centralises and preserves heroic decision-making. Established parties are in control but posture magnanimity and inclusion. Co-creation is a very different beast. It is indicative of a post-heroic approach because it exercises trust and responsibility. The post-heroic leader who works co-creatively, purposely develops teams and gives them genuine decision-making power. Such leaders trust the people they work with to trade beyond their experience, and in so doing open the doors to innovation beyond what currently exists.

Encouraging critical conversations

Another feature of the post-heroic leader is an ability to develop deeply critical conversations where respect for questioning and alternative solutions is attentively nurtured, even when such conversations challenge what seem like effective solutions. Saccharine dismissals like 'Thank you for sharing that', followed by a quick segue back to the intended trajectory of the discussion, are replaced by attentive inquiry. In such situations we generally encounter decentralised but critical questioning that explores what is being offered. Thus we might ask:

- What do you see as options for dealing with this problem?
- What is your preferred option and why?
- What are the benefits, costs and risks of this option?
- What would have to be done to execute your plan?
- Who else needs to be involved?
- What support would you need?

This type of critical questioning demonstrates an approach where initiatives are viewed in terms of strategic empowerment.

Changing heroic practices

The fourth feature relates to the way post-heroic leaders strategically change practices that continue to emphasise the heroic model of leadership. They change the ineffective by relentlessly infecting it with more empowering approaches. When they enter an established hierarchy they behave disobediently. This subversion, when well handled, becomes viral because others witness effective change and it empowers them to either take control of their own leadership potential or to question systems that keep them constrained. Because such infection is positive and inclusive, people are attracted to it. It demonstrates, in living ways, how more people can feel valued more of the time.

In my experience such infections are rarely epic in nature. They are an accumulation of small, intimately felt shifts in the levels of trust and value we feel. On personal levels they cause us to experience better things and consequently generate higher expectations of the organisations in which we work. But very small initiatives can be powerful. Let me give you an example.

Some years ago I worked at a teachers' college. While in truth I found the place a little too beige for my taste, I encountered within it some excellent leaders. One, who held a significant position, had a distinctive approach to meetings. Traditionally we are summoned into the offices of those above us on the hierarchy, but if you made an appointment with this guy he wanted to come and talk with you in the place where you were working. He told me once he thought people were more empowered and less threatened on their home territory. He believed colleagues were less likely to be inauthentic, and by joining them in their world he believed that he gained insights into the perspectives they experienced.

Despite this predilection for visiting, he did have an office, but it was somewhere he went in order to do paperwork or meet outside visitors. What I remember is that he knew a great deal more about his organisation than most leaders I have worked with – and people liked him.

Such decentralised approaches have their parallels in leaders who purposely operate horizontally. They physically work 'with' rather than 'above' their colleagues. In making a conscious effort to be an invited part of our world, they help to incrementally even out rituals of privilege. Such people rarely sit at the head of a table, have a privileged carpark or display ostentatious signifiers of status. They generally ask our advice or recommend colleagues who they believe have greater insights than they do. Most importantly, they undermine the damage of self-heroism by operating as an attentive enabler and appreciator of the people around them.

Storying change

And there is one last thing. The most effective post-heroic leaders I know are strategic storytellers. They know that change must have a voice. Accordingly, they change antithetical systems by recognising and disseminating authentic stories of success achieved by people with whom they work. Their own name rarely appears in such narratives. When leaders actively 'story' successes and attribute them to others, those who contributed to the change feel valued and more willing to increase their commitment. By storying well, they become change agents who erode myths of disempowerment and cultures of dismissal. Because they seem to understand implicitly Ben Okri's observation that 'Stories are always a form of resistance,'[57] they become very good at reconfiguring environments by infecting them with well-promoted examples of other people's positive alternatives.

thorns in the bed of roses

Of course post-heroic leadership sounds wonderful, but it is no bed of roses. When we choose to activate change in education through the empowerment of others, we ask people to shift deeply embedded cultures of practice that for some have become not only ritualised but also comfortable retreats from responsibility. Whether in an office or in a classroom, the post-heroic leader's disobedience becomes disruptive to a learned order. If you are such a leader, when you seek to change the dynamics of a hierarchy you probably face two significant challenges. The first involves negotiating your positional role, and the second relates to problems that occur when you increase the burden of responsibility for the people with whom you operate.

The positional role

Irrespective of what sort of educator you are, you have the authority to make decisions for the groups you develop. Whether you set up a system where students increasingly co-create the parameters, content and learning emphasis of their projects, or you guide an institution through a major transition, you are ultimately responsible for your decisions and the people who place their trust in you. There is nothing soft about post-heroic leadership. At the end of the day you, along with your decisions, are on the mat. If the paradigm shift you suggest fails, you can take down the dreams of those who trusted you. In addition, you are often operating in antithetical environments, and the nature of your leadership has to be carefully considered and tenacious.

In the 1990s I worked in a school that was undergoing a very profound shift in culture. Its falling roll and diminishing effectiveness had marked it for closure. A new principal had been appointed, and he brought with him a very different form of leadership. Although he wouldn't have defined himself as post-heroic, you could use the term to describe the way that he worked. He was a guy who clearly understood his positional role and responsibilities, and he negotiated these with great care – and this was difficult. Two small incidents and one enduring attitude marked him out as a post-heroic leader.

On the day he arrived he took a device off his office door. It was an electronic system that told people when the principal was available for appointments. It had stopped working years before and was jammed on the word 'engaged'. The device symbolically operated as a reminder that the principal was not to be disturbed. He also took down the sign saying 'principal' and put up one with his name on it. Finally, he wedged his office door open.

The second incident occurred some time later. Because he was a leader who spent a lot of time with his colleagues he was often away from his office. Some months after he took up his position, representatives from the Ministry of Education arrived, and when he couldn't be found they were directed into the school grounds. They searched the library and the assembly hall and in frustration, because their time was limited, they finally approached the guy weeding a garden over by the incinerator. They asked him if he was the caretaker and he smiled and said that he was. Using the opportunity to gain some insight into grass-roots changes, they began a polite conversation, asking him how things had altered in the school. He was an affable guy who not only told them how he had water-blasted off the signs indicating parking areas reserved for senior staff, but also about the working parties that had been set up to change systems of accountability in the school. He knew all of the staff and all of the kids and all of the buildings. He told them which grounds needed developing and why they needed to invest in a new technology block and what would make for better planting along the road front. In the end he offered to introduce them to a teacher who was taking an English lesson on kite flying out on the rugby field. Circumventing his enthusiasm, they politely drew their conversation to a close by asking him if he knew where they could find the principal. He looked at them for a moment, then smiled and held out his hand. He said if they gave him a moment to clean up, he could meet them in the staff room for a cuppa.

Such stories become legends in schools because they are indicative of difference. When I meet colleagues who worked with this principal they still recall his 'caretaking' role. He is remembered fondly, but not only because of euphoric stories about his modesty. He is also remembered for being a very, very strong man.

It is the nature of effective leaders that they must be both tenacious and deeply responsible. This is because the environments they seek to reform can be oppositional. The school this guy arrived in had an entrenched power structure that was maintained by a small number of senior staff whose privileges and ineptitude ran very deep. While superficially welcoming him, they soon recognised that his propensity to empower other people was very threatening. Across three years they worked unrelentingly to undermine what he was doing. They held back information, they bullied those they saw as subordinates and they engineered letters of complaint from parents and staff. They also sensed, very early, the vulnerability such a leader faces when working with empowerment. Hierarchical systems are very easy to maintain. You tell people what to do and they do it because you are the boss. The relationship between your position and how you use power is simply constructed. People do what they are told. You don't have to justify yourself because you are higher up than they are.

But for post-heroic leaders things aren't that straightforward. Such people need to constantly balance positions of responsibility with opening up opportunities. When you have to call an individual or group to account, you can be accused of undermining the values of empowerment you are working hard to establish. In exercising responsibility you can be accused of hypocrisy.

But the plain fact is, we are responsible and we are placed in a position where we are expected to exercise this responsibility. As post-heroic leaders we have to stand up to opposition when it disempowers other people or subverts transparency. Over the five years I worked with the 'caretaking' principal I watched him stand up to incredible opposition. He confronted a senior manager he saw bullying a younger teacher in a corridor. Despite the shouting, abuse and threats he ordered him back to his office until he calmed down, then insisted on a facilitated meeting of apology to his colleague.

He stopped a meeting where a staff member had smuggled in a tape recorder to gather incriminating evidence against a colleague and he insisted that she reveal what she was doing. He stood up to delegations of parents whose kids were being held accountable for bullying even when they threatened to bring in lawyers. He was calm, and clear, and very tenacious. When newspapers came to write stories on him, he consistently directed them away from his office and over to teachers working in the school. He would ask advice of colleagues, empower them to change things and then defer to their opinions. Needless to say, a great many leaders surfaced through that school, both students and staff. In addition, very talented people applied to work there because it was increasingly seen as a place where you could operate as a leader, where you would be trusted, and where you were expected to assume responsibility for your actions. Across a decade the school changed phenomenally. Not because of one heroic leader, but because of an environment he and a community of other leaders grew. But at the base of this was a guy who knew that he had a position. He accepted the responsibilities that went with this and he didn't back down when it came to defending the values that underpinned it.

The burden of responsibility

Balancing the empowerment of others and the responsibilities of one's position is a challenge. But there is a second problem facing the post-heroic leader. This is the fact that not everybody wants the increased burden of responsibility involved in working in non-hierarchical environments. Some individuals nurtured for years in traditional systems don't want to be suddenly held responsible for their decisions, and they object when it becomes harder to slip beneath the sweep of the radar. Hierarchical systems can be comfortable because they eventually hold somebody higher up in the system accountable for our actions. We can securely criticise what happens because we are rarely expected to actually stand for anything beyond arranging that things on our level run with minimal disruption. We simply supply what was contracted. In such systems things are pretty much cut and dried. The teacher is the boss, they take control of the class, they implement the learning that matters, and they tell the students what they need to do to get good marks. Students don't have to take the risks and they are not responsible for ideas that don't work.

When we turn this upside down we ask people to take responsibility for their contributions and we expect a deeper investment. In asking others to co-create the world in which they learn, we introduce instability and expectation into a safe, comparatively low-maintenance environment. I once learned this lesson brutally from a classroom of secondary school students.

the nature of brick walls

At the end of the 1980s I was working in a school where a wide range of educational experiments were being trialled, some surfacing from quite different philosophical bases. I had been teaching there for three years and I had become increasingly concerned about how little our students were expected to take responsibility for what and how they learned. Edging their way through a predetermined system they had become bored and dismissive, and if they were focused it was normally only on what was needed for a good mark. I caught myself using assessment as a way of eliciting motivation that I knew should be inherent in the learning process. It felt bad, so I decided to do something about it.

I began rethinking how I might approach the way I taught. From my years as a primary school teacher I knew that students were far more motivated when they could construct their own projects. I had seen how they would work harder and more authentically when they could feel their soul in the content of what they were doing. I also knew that the obsession with marking was hugely damaging. So I constructed an alternative approach. It was based on the following five observations.

- People prefer to create when learning.
- The resources of 25 people are greater than the resources of one.
- People will take risks if you take away assessment.
- People prefer to solve problems than to receive solutions.
- People will put an inordinate amount of effort into ideas or solutions that they believe are unique to themselves.

I set up a new sixth form course called visual communication. It was a programme nestled somewhere between design, English, art and technology. The subject was developed to be entirely project-based and students would work with blocks of time to set projects for themselves. There would be no marks given during the year; instead, marks would be replaced by peer critique at the end of each project. I would teach the students how to develop these skills and how to design two illustrated self-reports that would be available for their parents and the school (this was a requirement the principal had placed on the programme). Most importantly, though, the course would be something the students co-created. We would discuss the broad skills they needed to work with and they would design how they learned them. In my naivety I thought the approach would be greeted with open arms.

Fired with enthusiasm, over the summer holidays I replaced the graffitied desks in my classroom with new tables made of custom-wood packing sheets. I sewed up some huge cushions to reduce the amount of formal seating, and I bought a sofa from a second-hand shop. There were façades of plywood flying fish, windsongs and giant papier-mâché palm trees. To break up the spaces in the room I hung banners of printed cloth from the ceiling. Then I suspended posters and strange objects from nylon string. By February, with the ambient music and potted plants it looked and felt more like a budget Home Show than a classroom.

There was no teacher's desk positioned by the heater with the softest chair and a commanding view of the back-wall displays. I would sit at the same level as the students, wherever there was a spare seat. I could teach and question and listen from anywhere in the room.

On the first day of school the students bundled in. I felt proud and excited. They gazed around the room, wide eyed and open mouthed, laughing nervously and making tentative moves over to the sofa. As they circled the tables I listened and watched them. This was new territory. There weren't enough desks or enough cushions for a full set of anything. They asked me if the sofa was for the teacher.

After a few minutes most of them drifted over to the cushions and I settled down with them. We were splayed across the floor in a tangled kind of circle, 25 students and a nervous teacher. Rachel, the star of the school's swimming team, had already commandeered five pillows and was looking for another. Other kids were sitting on the carpet. Although I had taught most of them before, the traditional boundaries had gone. This was going to be a testing time. I wanted to see if they would be prepared to change the way they learned things.

I opened my knapsack and took out a paper bag. Then I asked them what they thought was inside it. In true adolescent fashion they quickly identified it as food. They suggested oranges and grapes and a range of more exotic possibilities. With the wind taken out of my sails I reached in and pulled out a solitary apple. It was one of those over-red, over-waxed ones that you sometimes find in the supermarket; the type they have kids crunching into on the television commercials. I placed it on the floor in front of us and produced a pocketknife. Then I asked them a question: 'If we've only got this one apple, and 25 kids, what's the best way of sharing it out?'

A few eyebrows superciliously swept the ceiling.

I picked up the apple and pulled out the stalk. 'No, it's not health education,' I said. 'Look at it. It's school. It's the big prize. The one teacher, the one resource. How are you going to share it out among 25 kids?'

Rachel looked up from her mound of cushions. 'Cut it up,' she said. 'Share it out evenly so everybody gets some.' (The others glanced at her pillows.)

'That's great,' I said. 'But what if somebody didn't have breakfast this morning? What if someone is more hungry than everyone else?'

'Tough.'

Sean pulled some fluff off the carpet. 'You could just let everybody take what they needed,' he said.

'Yeah,' said Rachel, 'and it would be woofed down in the first few minutes.' She settled back into her padded mound.

'Well, is there another way?' I asked.

'You could just put it in the middle of the floor,' suggested Matt, 'and tell people to go for it. You know … the survival of the fittest.'

Everybody laughed.

'Well that's what happens,' he said.

'But that wouldn't be fair,' said Rachel.

He looked at her.

Then Natasha spoke: 'I suppose you could all sit down and work out how much everybody needed. Then you could just divide it up. It would be fairer than just cutting it up evenly.'

'Will that work?' I asked.

Sean glanced up. 'Only in the textbooks,' he said. 'If people are hungry, they're going to take what they can. They're not going to talk about it.'

'Okay. So what are we left with then? We've got all of these ways of dividing up an apple, and that's fine if it's just an apple, but what if we call it education? Which of these methods of sharing out is going on in schools now?'

They began to stop shuffling and you could see them thinking.

'Is it the one where everybody gets equal time?' I said.

There was a ripple of laughter, ironic, and no agreement.

'Well, is it the one where people get what they need?'

They looked at each other and then Semisi spoke. 'No,' he said, 'that's how they say it is, but it's not really what happens. If you're dumb or quiet, you get ignored.'

'Well, what about the survival of the fittest one?' I asked. 'Is that what happens?'

The laughter rippled out again and several people began to speak at once. It was obvious this had struck a raw nerve.

'Not the survival of the fittest,' said Meri. 'The survival of the most demanding. You don't get marks for helping somebody else.'

'Are you sure?' I said. 'Isn't that just painting ourselves as the victims?'

'Bullshit!' said Rachel. 'It's what happens! It's the competition. You've got to compete with each other for everything. Nobody shares things out when you compete. That sharing and caring stuff is just crap. It's all a fancy cover teachers put on things, but underneath they're still looking for the best.'

There was silence for a moment and I looked around the group. Pita was glancing out of the window. This wasn't what he'd come here for.

'What if I could show you another way,' I said, 'where you wouldn't have to compete with each other and could still get as much of the apple as you need?'

Rachel looked up. 'Yeah,' she said, 'in your dreams.'

'Yes. In your dreams but, also in reality. There's another way of learning.'

Matt leaned over and picked up the apple. 'Yeah, but there's still only one of these.'

'You're right.' I said. 'But that's the point. There doesn't have to be just one apple. You can have as many apples as you want. The only difference is that you learn how to make them for yourself. You would set up your own learning. You would assess yourselves. The class would become like a big co-operative.'

At this point it was all playing out like a great educational video. The apple had worked itself overtime and the kids were thinking about how they learned. Then something hit the fan, and it wasn't soft. It was reality. It came with a crunching sound that ground the euphoria to a halt. It was Rachel, who woke up to the implications of what was being suggested.

'So who would mark us?' she asked.

'No-one. You would get feedback instead.'

'But what good's that?' asked Matt. 'How would you know if you were failing?'

'You wouldn't fail. I wouldn't let you,' I said. 'You'd get more help because it wouldn't just be a grade or a percentage. I would be more like a coach than a teacher. I would go over what needed to be learned in each project and you could work out how you wanted to do it. The decision-making would be back in your hands. You would put all of your work together at the end of the year, after you had lots of feedback and opportunities to redo stuff, then there would be just the one mark the government insists on. Just one. At the end. You and I could do this bit together. Everything leading up to that would be you setting your assignments and getting feedback from the other people in the group.'

Rachel was incredulous. 'But that's not our job. You're the one who's paid to do that.'

I was shocked. I had spent three years listening to these same kids moaning about how irrelevant their assignments were and how unfair the marking was. I thought they would be glad to be in the driving seat of their own learning.

'But wouldn't you rather write your own assignments?' I asked.

Rachel had now flustered herself up into a flurry of indignation. 'But I don't have time to do all of this,' she said. 'I have swimming practice.'

I looked around. It was clear she wasn't the only one thinking this way. I tried another approach. 'But it would be more relevant, wouldn't it? If you could take responsibility – if you could decide how you learn.'

Meri was polite. She carefully explained the fundamentals as if I were a child. 'No. It's not like that. We need good marks. We need to know where we're going. You need to tell us.'

God! I couldn't believe I was hearing this. Nothing in the euphoric books on teaching reform mentioned this part of the story.

'Anyway', added Sean, 'we're not teachers. It just sounds like a lot of work for something that mightn't work.'

I watched as the initiative began to slide down its first brick wall. I had missed something important. I hadn't understood that these students had been shaped by 12 years inside a comfortable, hierarchical system that rewarded them based on their ability to dance to somebody else's tune. They only knew external approval. Risk and responsibility may have sounded great, but these kids had been trained to be risk averse. They weren't buying it. They were afraid.

With the moral fibre of a tabloid talk-show host I changed gear and started lying. Well, perhaps it wasn't lying, but it wasn't the unassailable truth. I promised things I wasn't sure I could deliver. I told them if passing was important then I would make sure, if they did all of the work, that they wouldn't fail. I felt like an ideological traitor. I reminded them of our shared experience of learning together over three years. They knew I was tough and they knew that I cared about them.

So, eventually, with the provision that after the first project we could throw the idea out if it didn't work, we edged forward. The approach became an exercise in trust. I had to trust them to tell me what was working and they had to trust me to be a good coach.

aftermaths

I can't claim to have got everything right. The students worked hard and a plethora of projects were undertaken. By popular demand each year the number of classes I taught doubled. But like many post-heroic reformers I talked with in later years, I had to come to terms with the fact that sometimes we were on a journey without a road map. I also learned that I was flawed, and so were kids – and so were some dreams.

Over time I came to understand the importance of strength. I had to show the classes how they could develop group feedback skills so their critique sessions were neither disabling nor passively euphoric. I had to learn to stand up for things when other people couldn't. I had to work with groups so they learned to hold their peers accountable. I rapidly realised that when working post-heroically you have to understand systems and learn how and why they function the way they do. But there was one thing I didn't see coming.

It was the toxicity of success.

In the four years during which the teaching initiative developed, summative assessment was pushed to the outer perimeter. There was only one non-peer assessment per year, and this was the external one required to meet New Zealand Qualifications

Authority requirements. The kids were adamant that they didn't have time for subjects that wouldn't produce a final 'useable' grade. I learned (reluctantly) to compromise. As the approach grew, we also applied this way of learning to the way the art, design and technology curriculums were taught.[58] This felt good, because it showed that increasingly the kids could see the benefit of an alternative approach. However, when the results of the examinations became public, the marks wreaked havoc on the initiative.

You see the grades were an anomaly, because each year the students ranked well above the national average.[59] I was happy they did well, but to me the marks they scored were only a byproduct of something far more important. All these grades indicated was that, even under the most traditional and antithetical method of measuring, people still performed significantly better in a system they could co-create. The relationships developed between learners, the personalised nature of the commitment and the ability to manage complex projects and critically appraise their own work were the real sources of success. But most of the kids didn't realise this yet. They didn't know that their ability to take control of their learning would in the long run be the most useful thing they gained.

In the end the power of the successful mark proved a very tough beast to keep under control. Doing well in exams still meant a lot to the students, and it was hard to convince people that these grades were not a vindication of the approach. As word got out, each year increasing numbers of ambitious students swapped schools to join the classes. But for many of these new kids and their parents the driving force behind their espoused enthusiasm for an alternative was really just the desire for a higher grade. I discovered that an initiative like this could end up turning back on itself. Against everything I had believed and had tried to marginalise, the power of the external mark became an unwanted beacon at the door.

Over time the demographic characteristics of the classes changed. The new students wanted the cool veneer of an alternative, but they and their parents also wanted reports from the teacher. They wanted assurance. They wanted success and monitoring. In the end they insisted on things that I felt I could no longer give them. I still hadn't learned how to work with change well enough to find my way around what was happening. I had come up against something very fundamental: sometimes people prefer to work with the rhetoric of self-responsibility rather than its substance.

In this period of my teaching I learned the dangers of success. What constitutes success is based on deeply embedded values. If we still believe (somewhere way down there) that marks indicate achievement, then when grades go public we can end up accepting them as a kind of validation. Even if we don't, we have to cope with the fact that others will. This can be very disorienting if our educational motivations are based on something more insightful.

The seduction of success is pernicious because we are vulnerable when we operate at the vanguard of change. It is easy to lose our way in the glow of acclaim and compliments. But if people appreciate what we do for false reasons, and we acquiesce, we can end up demobilising ourselves. This is what happened to me. In my naivety I hadn't understood that conservative systems can neutralise change by framing the outcomes of productive disobedience as a glorified *exception*. Our initiatives become pampered anomalies, not accommodated as viable alternatives. Our disobedience is spoken about endearingly, but it is tolerated only for so long as it earns something that obedience can't. In the euphoria of its success a little token space is made for us and it feels warm and welcoming. It is very hard to look into the face of such acknowledgement and explain that things still aren't right – and then to turn around and walk back to the problems of the chalk face.

My only salvation when this happened came from the kids I taught. I knew that stories told about the success were edited. I remembered that Edward danced his Ballet of Pavlov's dogs in these classes. He left school unhappy and defeated. I had students who had been expelled from other schools and adults who were returning to school in a desperate effort to undo the damage that had been done to their self-esteem years earlier. They showed me that change isn't heroic. It takes tenacity and a grasp on both hope and your moral compass. I learned that real change is incremental. Its roots lie in understanding how people value things, not in the sweeping revolution in a brightly coloured classroom. Peer assessment and glowing portfolios don't overthrow hierarchical education systems or the values they generate. What effects change, no matter how small, is an investment in people and being aware of the consequences of what we do. True reform has to wash its face in the mirror every morning. It has to look up and make contact with its fundamental values, even while there are people applauding in the background.

So I have learned that enduring change is not a revolutionary coup: it is human. The change of human beings is far more influential and profound than the change of systems, and I settle for this because it is deeper. Knowing how systems operate is important, but at the heart of reform lies something stronger and more precious. It is non-heroic, enabling and optimistic. It works like a virus. It infects with hope and it supports people's ability to transform the world in which they operate.

This singular understanding that change comes from working at a personal level is stronger than any structural revolution on earth.

* * *

PART SIX

INFLUENCING CHANGE

an anomaly on flight A320

Some years ago I was on a flight to Wellington for a symposium for educators who had received national awards for their teaching. I had been told that there would be five other colleagues on the airline, but I didn't know any of them. To be honest I was feeling a bit awkward. I find events related to any sort of accolade a bit difficult.

In a disruption to the norm I ended up among the first people seated on the aeroplane, so because I am easily amused I decided to play a game. I tried to work out if I could identify these 'wonder teachers' among the 150 other passengers. I guess I was being a bit cynical, but, you know, the strangest thing happened. I identified every one of them, and for the most wonderful reasons. When one by one they bundled onto the plane they were already in conversation with a stranger, they laughed and helped people with their luggage. They checked that those around them were okay before jovially climbing into their seats. They were full of enthusiasm.

But what was most distinctive was the way they devoted so much emphasis to listening to whatever person they were in conversation with. It was very distinctive. They appeared to be absorbed, and I suspect that they genuinely were.

Over the two-day conference I discovered that this was a highly distinctive bunch of people: idiosyncratic, joyful, brave, committed, innovative and full of foibles. Perhaps Abraham Maslow would have called them self-actualised, but I just thought of them as likeable, outwardly focused individuals. They had a palpable dislike of over-systematised processes and they were hugely supportive of each other. These teachers were genuinely wonderful people.

I came away wondering how it was that such co-operative, thoughtful, slightly eccentric individuals should be the ones who rose to the top of a teaching environment that is so predicated on competition, standardisation and systematised measurement. I realised that I was in the presence of an anomaly.

at the base of everything

When I thought about it, though, I realised that these teachers were indicative of something I have recognised across 55 years inside school systems. What they shared was an ability to change things and make them better. By this I mean they didn't wait for permission to try out ideas. They didn't give up in the face of opposition. They made mistakes, because we all do. But if something could be done, then they tried it, and they used a professionally refined compass to find their way through possibility. They were all by nature disobedient. They closed classroom doors when necessary and used what they co-created with their students to infect the broader environment in which they worked. But their ideas took root because they had an unrelenting commitment to a belief in the potential of people. Underneath this lay a tacit understanding of one very fundamental truth, very simple but very profound. These teachers knew that people need to feel valued. If they feel valued, you can get them to change.

Understanding and knowing how to work with this idea is a very powerful thing. Partly this is because when we understand how to value people and work out how to express this in genuine ways, they want to work with us. If this sounds simplistic, it's not.

Today I do consultancy work with a wide range of organisations and businesses, both in New Zealand and overseas. Most of these institutions are trying to find better ways to attract and grow talented people. Their effective leaders – the ones who engender trust and move change forward – have as their primary skill the ability to understand and work with other people. This is because no matter how complex an organisation is, it is only *people* who can change it. The only things that are living in institutions are the individuals who populate them. An organisation's potentials and blockages are human. Its stories of dissatisfaction and conflict are human, and its hopes and aspirations are human. It doesn't matter how much energy is expended talking about vision and identity and the nature of the corporate brand: all institutions are populated, shaped and transformed by human beings. Once we learn to work with them and their motivations, our ability to change worlds becomes infinitely more effective.

I'm not going to pretend that there is a list of easily acquired behaviours that will give you this. The ability to change people and systems is a complex and at times idiosyncratic thing. But there do appear to be a number of behaviours that are found among genuinely influential leaders. Teachers who have these skills transform students, and they have the power to change schools, communities and wider educational ways of understanding. Their influence can run very deep and cross generations. On the surface some of the qualities I am going to discuss may look strange, but they are all linked back to the single understanding that people will do things that make them feel valued.

Let's start with a seemingly odd one.

don't criticise

I have discovered that it is never effective to criticise people. On the surface this may sound silly. We are taught that 'telling it like it is' is the mark of a strong person. Well, that may be true, but it isn't the mark of an influential person. Changing people takes considerably more skill than shooting from the hip. If you think about it, very rarely do we respond well to criticism. We might magnanimously thank a critic for their opinion, but deep down we feel that they didn't understand us. Nobody likes being told they are wrong.

I remember once working with the manager of a major distributing company who was frustrated because he couldn't get the people he worked with to take risks. He saw himself as a good boss and he was proud of his direct approach. He was honest and forthright, and he comforted himself with the assurance that everybody knew where they stood. And this was true. Everybody knew exactly where they stood, and in general if they were forced to take a risk it was as far away from him as possible. Why?

He was very critical. He gave advice about how the situation should have been dealt with and he explained the solution. Many of his answers may have been right, but that wasn't what people remembered. What they remembered was that the cost of taking initiative is criticism.

So, we might ask, what is more effective than criticism? It is helping people to come up with solutions themselves. Great teachers do this all the time. They coax, encourage, question and reward, and by doing this they help students discover what they didn't know. Effective leaders do it when they grow high-calibre organisations. Such reformers recognise that people will automatically choose to be part of a solution rather than be criticised. But often criticising feels much faster and more effective. We find what's wrong, we tell the person what it is, then we tell them to fix it. All done!

Well, probably *not* all done at all. In fact it's likely that very little has been done. The behaviour may have changed, but the only things that will have really happened will be a reconfirmation of disempowerment and a subtle increase in resentment.

But certain people are very good at working beyond criticism. Although almost apocryphal now, I remember the story of Bob Hoover's air crash as a graphic example. Hoover was one of the founders of modern aerobatics. One day he was returning to Los Angeles after a flying demonstration in San Diego. Cruising at 300 feet with two passengers, he suddenly experienced a pilot's worst nightmare. Both engines cut out. While the plane plummeted he frantically engineered the descent and when they crashed he was able to save both his life and those of his two companions. But the vehicle was destroyed. When he inspected the wreckage he discovered that he had been flying with jet fuel instead of gasoline.

When Hoover returned to the airport where the vehicle had been fuelled up he asked to see the young mechanic who had serviced the plane. The man was deeply distressed and apologising profusely. His mistake had caused the destruction of an expensive aeroplane and the near death of its three occupants. But Hoover was an interesting man. Instead of criticising, he did something very distinctive. He put his arm around the mechanic's shoulder and asked what had happened. He listened patiently, then he said,

'To show you I'm sure that you'll never do this again, I want you to service my F-51 tomorrow'.

One's loyalty to such a man would be profound. Hoover knew that real change happens voluntarily. It comes as an offering, not as compliance. If people are criticised they may submit to change but rarely is anything shifted. Because of the way he approached this situation, Hoover and his flights were now in the safest hands imaginable. He knew the transformative power of showing belief in people.

By avoiding criticising we can also emphasise trust and responsibility. Most of us can identify when we have done something wrong, and if someone can manoeuvre things so we can find a bridge back and dig ourselves out of the problem, we will take it. Naming, shaming and blaming only provides validation for the accusers; it is never the solution to a problem. I have learned over time when working with people who have made mistakes to stress that I am not interested in blaming them; I am only interested in their advice because we need to work out how we can ensure the situation can't happen again.

If we want to move people beyond flawed behaviour, we can't strip them of their dignity. They have to be able to preserve their sense of being valued. But just giving them space to find a solution doesn't always sort things on its own. Although asking them for advice about the best solution to their problem is invariably more effective than criticising, there is an additional skill that effective reformers use to achieve this. It is the ability to question.

question bravely

I have found that people who effect a lot of change are generally very good at asking questions, both of themselves and of others.

When I first started teaching I thought questioning was what you did to find the right answer in a class. Certainly this was the model I had seen on the movie screens and on the covers of all of my teaching textbooks. Good questioning meant a happy class, with their hands raised in enthusiasm and a beaming teacher. Of course this is nonsense.

Questioning is a complex skill that we use to assist people to think about things. It helps them to dig into what is not being thought so they can find solutions. Whether this happens in a classroom or with colleagues, how and when we ask questions is integral to how deeply we can transform something.

I have noticed when I watch great teachers that they generally behave inquisitively around people, and they ask questions as a way of helping others to clarify their ideas. They ask us *why* we think something happens, or *how* a solution might be improved, or *what* is working with a process. Questioning insightfully, then strategically reflecting back responses, stimulates analysis and moves people beyond passive reception.

Such questioning is a powerful skill that is used by effective leaders as a way of getting others to think critically about situations. These leaders question because they understand that not asking questions preserves damaging cultures. We know that the preservation of our own worst behaviours depends upon us *not* asking ourselves honestly what is going on and why we are not taking responsibility for it. Our contracted agreement to abstain from asking questions lets the behaviour maintain its hold on our lives.

It is also through this lack of courageous questioning that poor teachers and managers are able to remain in their positions. You can introduce systems that ask them to demonstrate as many performance indicators as you like, but without rigorous questioning they need only cosmeticise and report what is minimally necessary; then they can continue to operate in damaging ways. To keep an illusion of their effectiveness in place, they nurture contracts of silence with colleagues. Not surprisingly, such people can also become disparaging of rigorous feedback systems and feel very threatened when, despite their use of belittlement, obstruction or bullying, those around them refuse to retreat into silence.

Being courageous enough to question things that are not right is pivotal to effecting change. But it is difficult, and we often find ourselves trying to deal with issues in an environment where others who agree with us in private won't publically stand beside us. This is tough. But if we don't question, nothing will change. At the risk of proselytising, let me repeat that. *If we don't question, nothing will change.*

There is nothing new about this observation. Theodore DeVries noted, 'If we stand for nothing we will stand for anything'. Damaged environments – be they classrooms, schools or organisations – are populated with people who have been trained not to question. Instead, they are seduced into criticising in discreet, ineffectual, disgruntled pockets, but they do not influence change. By refusing to question, they actually reinforce the contract of silence and add to its strength.

When we question what exists, we suggest that things are open to change. We position ourselves above ideas and the systems they are used to create. Major reformers who have helped to profoundly change negative environments have all actively defied cultures of non-questioning. They unrelentingly broke contracts of silence. Whether these were political activists (Nelson Mandela, Martin Luther King, Aung San Suu Kyi), philosophers (Socrates, Voltaire), social reformers (Emmeline Pankhurst, Te Puea Herangi), scientists (Copernicus, Galileo, Alfred Wegener, Albert Einstein), religious critics (Maximilian Kolbe, Dietrich Bonhoeffer)[60] or educationalists (John Dewey, John Pounds, Maria Montessori), their diverse personalities and concerns shared this one feature in common. They all asked questions (unrelentingly) and they took action when other people didn't.

show an enduring interest in others

A third feature of the influential educator is an ability to show others that they matter. We are all interested in ourselves. In fact on any occasion the deepest needs and perspectives of the person you are talking to will always be their own. On any given day their health, stress, hopes and attitudes will come before whatever you bring in the door. When somebody greets us by name and enquires into something that demonstrates their interest in us an individual, we feel valued, because they show us that we matter.

I have a colleague who notes down the birthday of everybody he works with, and on that date he sends them a short email. For some people it is the only acknowledgement of their birthday they will get. His correspondence is not a generic thing. He always includes something unexpected in it, a small observation about what's going on in the person's life or a recommendation about something he thinks they might like. He is very popular because people feel that he is interested in them. He gets invited to more events than anyone else I know. He remembers people's names. He refers to things they have said or done and he is genuinely appreciative of anything they do for him. It is no surprise that he is extremely influential. I remember that I employed him on the recommendation of the tea lady.

When he applied for the job I was the acting head of a large school of design in a university. I worked with over 70 staff and together we sought to grow the potentials of up to a thousand students each year. As part of my position I had to interview people for what were highly sought-after positions. Hiring staff is always a complex undertaking because you are normally dealing with an artificial projection of identity. After the letters have been read, interview questions answered and CVs considered, you are left aware of just how limited such processes can be in determining someone's goodness. I say goodness because I have come to believe that this is central to a person being effective in an organisation. You can have talent and ambition, vision and strategy, but without an ethical heart and a genuine interest in other people, you can never really help them to extend their potential.

During this period there was an interesting phenomenon occurring just below my office. Downstairs a woman called Maureen had a little business, a café where she sold homemade cakes and served tea to the people working in the building. Every day the glass shelves of her counter were festooned with an array of offerings – bright pink lamingtons, chocolate slices and cheese scones straight out of childhood. Her sponges could set your teeth ringing at 40 paces. I loved Maureen. In fact everybody loved her.

Staff would migrate from other buildings just to buy her cakes and receive the small dose of motherly affection she served up with their morning coffee. We all knew about Maureen's cat and her husband's health and what she intended to pick up from the supermarket for tomorrow's offerings. In turn, she asked about our families and our gardens, and she would gently admonish us for working too hard. On days when she thought we were looking a bit under the weather she would cut an extra piece of cake and slip it surreptitiously onto our tray.

Maureen had the best human radar I have ever encountered. After interviewing an applicant and before deciding whether I should offer them a position, I would always take them down to her café for a cup of tea. While we waited in line I would continue talking with them. I knew as we approached the counter that Maureen's open nature and natural curiosity would cause her to interrupt and start a conversation.

How the person responded to her always told me a great deal about them. If they answered her questions briefly then quickly focused their attention back onto what we were discussing, Maureen would slice them a marginally smaller piece of cake, smile and subtly purse her lips, and we would leave the queue and finish our tea at one of the spare tables in her café. But if they responded to her warmth with similar generosity, they would instantly reveal something important about how they valued people.

Invariably the next time I dropped in for a cuppa Maureen would ask if I had appointed them. She read people very well. She didn't care about the weight of their CV or how well they delivered their responses to questions at an interview table. She cared about how they functioned as a human being.

Maureen knew that if you want success, you need to have successful relationships. Someone who builds great relationships appreciates others. When we are in their company they encourage us and we feel more enabled and confident. Conversely, when we work with someone who is critical and subtractive, we normally feel let down. People who influence people are able to master the art of building value in others. Such reformers know the importance of understanding another person's perspective. Their ability to enter situations with empathetic insight means they have a much higher chance of appreciating what is really going on. They can understand and work with the issues that motivate our behaviours.

think from the other person's perspective

A fourth feature of an influential leader is their ability to reorient their perspective. By this I mean they can consciously put themselves in other people's shoes. They know that the people they work with need to feel valued and they build motivation from this.

Many of the things I have changed in my time in education have resulted from this simple understanding. If you want something to succeed, let other people take the credit. For instance, I have learned not to insist that an idea I introduce is attributed to me. If I want it to take root, I have to be prepared for other people to believe that it is theirs and to claim it as such. In fact, as they begin to develop it I will openly attribute it to them. This approach results in ideas growing faster, achieves higher levels of buy-in and helps people I am working with to feel valued. By extension, when engaged in discussions, I always make a point of mentioning an originator's name when I expand on an idea they have offered.

I have also learned to strategically support people when they are in a difficult situation. I have a friend who is very good at this. In meetings if she knows a vulnerable colleague is going to propose something or argue a point on which she agrees, she will sit opposite them at the table, in their direct line of sight. This way she says she can be sure that when they look up they will see somebody who agrees with them. She told me, if you sit next to them, although it may seem caring, they have to glance awkwardly sideways for assurance. By causing them to speak across the table you can help their presentation look more confident and inclusive.

Such behaviour is indicative of a thoughtfully reorienting personality. Such individuals consider situations from the other person's perspective so that they are able to change the emotional environment in which they operate. Thus, when attempting to facilitate open discussion, I try never to sit at the head of a table.

Such positioning subtly emphasises uneven authority. When somebody is distressed I avoid taking a seat that is higher than they are. By extension, my office is furnished with sofas – not because I see lounging as a professional activity, but because such seating is familiar. It says to people that no matter how difficult a situation is, you can relax. In such environments you can deal with very difficult issues because the world in which you work is welcoming and confident. You are humanised, and so – immediately – is the person who meets with you.

Such considerations may appear very small, but they have a profound effect. It was not with naivety that Winston Churchill noted, 'We shape our buildings, and afterwards our buildings shape us.'[61] Be they classrooms, offices or meeting rooms, we read spaces very quickly. We assess the dynamics of power within them and adjust ourselves accordingly.

But the ability to see from other people's perspectives operates beyond how we use space. When having to deal with potential conflict I try to prepare myself by thinking about what an opponent *needs* out of the situation. I am not talking here about what they *want*, but the deeper *need* they have. This means understanding the motivation behind the position they are adopting.

A few years ago I was chairing a PhD examination. The candidate was very nervous, and in my briefing with him a week earlier he had become very defensive. One of the three examiners, whose report he had received, was highly critical of his literature review. The candidate did not know at this point that the examiner wanted to fail the thesis, but he was preparing to enter the two-hour oral defence with all guns blazing. He thought the examiner had been unfair and he was going to deal with her in no uncertain terms.[62]

In the days leading up to the examination I gave the situation a lot of thought. I realised that beneath the examiner's concerns lay the fact that her own research had not been cited, whereas certain theorists she disliked had been included and discussed in depth. The candidate's model had ignored her altogether. Although the other two examiners had assessed the thesis as well constructed, we were going to face a problem. I knew from past experience that if things come unstuck in an oral examination, years of study can end up in tatters on the carpet.

On the day of the event I set up the standard meeting with the examiners before the candidate entered the room. I welcomed them, thanked them for the thoroughness of their reports and out-lined the process we would follow. Then I took a moment to talk with them about the constitution of the panel. I noted that each examiner had been selected because she or he was considered a world leader in the field, and each of them came from different and sometimes opposing paradigms. I explained that the reason for their selection lay in their experience as examiners who had a proven record of being able to consider research from the position it adopted. I realised that finding examiners with this talent was not always possible, but in this instance I was looking forward to observing how they used the diversity of their viewpoints to help the candidate exhume the depth and quality of his research.

Then, just before the student entered, I mentioned as an aside that I had taken the liberty of reading some of their work. I explained (truthfully) that even though I came from a different discipline, I had found a recently published article by the woman examiner particularly helpful in my own research.

When the candidate entered the room he introduced himself and took five minutes to briefly outline his thesis. I had empha-sised to him, just prior to the meeting, that nobody was 'out to get him', but as seasoned academics they would be interested in the levelness and insight with which he answered their questions.

I can't pretend that it was an easy examination, but I had arranged that the first question would be relatively straightforward and it would be posed by one of the other examiners. At the end of two hours the panel unanimously agreed to pass the thesis and recommended only minor amendments. Interestingly, these requested changes were not to the literature review. At the close of the event, when each assessor congratulated the candidate, the examiner I had been most concerned about was eloquent in explaining the complexity of the field and the need to be cognisant of the full breadth of current debates. She explained that she didn't adopt the same position as the candidate, but in a dispassionate analysis of his defence she considered his examination to be of a suitably high standard. Her summing up was very impressive.

In the end all parties left respecting each other. Each had demonstrated their finest qualities and the examination had been both insightful and rigorous. In truth, I suspect I was hardly noticed, and that is the way it should be. My job was simply to arrange a process where the deepest of considerations could operate in the best possible environment.

humanise what opposes

Our ability to influence situations is closely related to our ability to humanise the environments in which we operate. If we establish ourselves as human and concurrently humanise the things that oppose us, we activate a very powerful dynamic. As far back as the first century the Roman senator Tacitus recognised that if you want people to work with you, you need to make them like you. Moreover, he noted, 'It belongs to human nature to hate those you have injured.'[63] In other words, he knew that it is very unproductive to put people who oppose you in a position where they believe they have hurt you. Their unspoken guilt will burn the bridges they might have crossed to find their way back to a good working relationship. Tacitus knew that in the face of opposition you need to become as resiliently humane as possible. It is very hard to attack something that you understand or empathise with. This is why change has the greatest chance of occurring in an environment where people have been enticed into showing appreciation of each other, even when they disagree. If Tacitus's observation sounds a little abstract, let me illustrate it with a mistake I once made.

In 1981 I was teaching at a school in the heartland of the North Island. I had been reprimanded both by the local newspaper and by members of the School Committee for protesting against the Springbok tour. After leading what must have been the loneliest and most undocumented anti-apartheid march in the country down the main street of the town (there were only three of us), I was forbidden to mention the Springbok issue in my classes.

When I returned to work one Monday with a black eye and a torn ear after a protest at a Hamilton rugby match, all I could do was explain to the kids that I was exercising my right to an opinion. But this was a small town. News of the injury spread like wildfire. The next day a letter to the editor appeared in the local paper. It accused me of being a communist. When I returned home from school I found the walls of my house had been plastered with eggs. I was shocked. Wounded and angry, and believing the town to be pitched against me, I stomped down to the woodshed, pulled out a ladder, a bucket and a scrubbing brush and marched back to the front of the house.

When I arrived there were three of my neighbours waiting. Although they didn't agree with my stand against the rugby tour, they had turned up with buckets of warm water and high-alkaline detergent to help me clean the mess off. They told me not to use hot water because heat would cook the yokes into the paintwork. We scrubbed for about an hour then someone turned up with scones and a large pot of tea, and we sat on the carport roof and talked about the price of wool, and their kids, and we laughed about something that had happened at the primary school calf club. Nobody mentioned the eggs. They knew how deeply I was committed to teaching their kids, and that knowledge, I realised, had overridden any broader differences in opinion.

Such incidents never happened again. Those people who had criticised my political actions later became my staunchest advocates. I toured their kids through drama festivals and cross-country meets all over the North Island. When a play I wrote for the local drama club won the New Zealand Theatre Festival, they phoned the Wellington *Dominion* newspaper to tell them to write an article on the success because the local paper had refused to mention it.

In crossing a line from opposition to humane empathy we had learned to work productively together. Maybe I couldn't have discussed the subtleties of Tacitus's insights with them, but from that point on I knew I could count on their support and I learned to stop thinking of them as opponents.

the strength of one

And now to the final feature that all influential people have in common, be they teachers, students, administrators, parents or community leaders. It is a simple and profound quality. It enables people to change things where change was thought impossible. It moves obstacles and imagines horizons. What is it?

It is a deep and abiding belief in your potential.

The other day I was reading a book by Sylvia Ashton Warner. I have a very deep respect for teachers and the challenges they face, and great teachers fascinate me. Like all human beings Ashton Warner was flawed; she operated without a road map and her writing resonates with passion and idiosyncrasy. In her book *Myself* she talks about a fundamental quality of influential people. What she discusses has been noted by many writers – everyone from Samuel Johnson to Henrik Ibsen. It appears in theological texts and in pop songs; it permeates advice columns and television talk shows, and it is something we often lose faith in. She put it like this:

> *You must be true to yourself. Strong enough to be true to yourself. Brave enough to be strong enough to be true to yourself. Wise enough to be brave enough to be strong enough to shape yourself from what you actually are.*[64]

Yes, being true to yourself is fundamental to being able to change things, but it is easier to write about than to live. I am a lucky man because over the years I have had relationships with some wonderful reformers who have understood the importance of belief in themselves. I am not talking here about self-promoters, or self-aggrandisers, but men and women who have a very deep sense of knowing who they are and a belief in the value they can bring to the world. They draw strength and wisdom and humanity not from the approval and permission of others, but from an inner sense of being human and full of potential. These people are not always CEOs or principals or acknowledged change agents, but they do transform the worlds in which they live because they know their essence and draw courage from that.

To illustrate this I would like to tell you the stories of two quiet people. Both are teachers who have changed lives in very profound ways and both would be startled to find their stories in a book like this. But both have a very deep understanding of who they are in the world and their potential within it. They are a reminder to me that some of the most powerful change agents in education operate away from the limelight.

Isobel is a quiet woman whom you would probably describe as modest. She works in a large school and incrementally she has helped to build a very effective department. People like her. On the morning we met it had been raining. She told me that while she was walking to the bus stop she had noticed that washed out onto the footpath was an array of sodden worms. They were limp and destined to die. While she was waiting for the bus, she began bending down and one by one picking them up and putting them back on the grass verge. The people in the shelter watched her and finally one of them explained to her that it hardly mattered because there would be hundreds more such worms as soon as it started raining again. She didn't say anything for a moment, but then she replied meekly that for those worms at least she had done something that mattered.

As I listened to her I didn't have the heart to explain that there was a version of this tale where a guy picked up starfish on the seashore. It had been doing the rounds of educational writing for decades. But I am glad that I said nothing and just listened, because she paused for a moment, then turned to me and told me something profound. She said, 'In truth, you know, it wasn't that I was saving the worms that really mattered. It was that those people saw me saving the worms.'

I suddenly understood why this woman changed worlds. This was more than dogged benevolence. This was about a middle-aged woman putting herself at risk to make a point. No matter how small. She didn't care what other people thought of her. She knew that it isn't just tenacity but being *seen* to be tenacious that matters. She doggedly saved worms on rainy days, and through such small gestures she showed another way that we might be in the world.

The second story concerns Miss Bavine. When I was 15 I fell in love with her. Miss Bavine was my geography teacher and she wore a mini skirt. Well, that is how most of the boys at my high school remembered her, but I was in love with Miss Bavine for quite a different reason. In the final weeks of my fourth form year I had the dubious honour of being sprung pashing Trevor Pratley behind the school gymnasium. Okay, perhaps it had progressed a little further than pashing, but at Te Awamutu College this act of adolescent enthusiasm paralleled tearing the gates off the entry to hell. The story exploded through the school like an apocalyptic bomb. Up until that time Trevor and I had been the college's prize distance runners; we were heroes and within the tight framework of what was acceptable we were pampered and approved of. Suddenly our reputations slumped like tasered choirboys.

Trevor had the common sense to rapidly secure himself a girl-friend, get her pregnant and leave school. But I stayed on. I didn't have much choice, really. The only way out of small towns in those days was to get an education so you could scramble off the conveyer belt that recycled the other boys back on to their fathers' farms or into local businesses.

What followed the gym incident was relatively predictable and most kids who have been bullied at school will have similar stories. Because I never tried to deny that I was gay I became the school homo. This meant having the contents of your school bag sprayed with pink paint, your lunch box filled with excrement and your phys ed gear constantly thrown into the girls' changing sheds. In such situations you learn very quickly to laugh, because if you don't people will see how effective they are and it will get much worse. You also learn that it's important to be late to class.

If you can't get to a classroom before everybody else arrives, you need to wait. Miss Bavine's geography lessons were no exception.

The teacher's admonishment was always better than climbing two flights of steps and dodging the sandwiches and insults the kids threw down on you. By coming in late you could also manage to avoid the populated doorway where the jostling and shoving happens in such a way that nobody can ever quite identify who has done it. So the pattern goes: you arrive late, the teacher asks if you have a note, you say no, and you get a detention. It's a small price, really.

But I was aware that Miss Bavine never questioned me. I thought perhaps she knew what was going on but being unable to stop it she did what most teachers did and ignored it. However, an incident that changed my life happened in her classroom in the period after lunch. The preceding day we had all sat a test on rainfall patterns in the South Island and Miss Bavine had spent the first five minutes of the lesson handing back our marks. Most of us had failed, but that was to be expected. We were in 5RB, the class for those expected to fail School Certificate the first time round and be back the following year for a second go. The 'R' stood for 'returns'. My marks weren't good. Like most of the kids I was just happy to occasionally scape through so I could hold on to the hope of having a shot at School Certificate at the end of the year. I don't remember much about the lesson, but I guess it ticked on like most of the others. We copied down notes and drew diagrams and looked out of the windows.

When the period ended and the bell rang everybody bundled out of the class. A few hung back, mainly for the sport of it. I think Miss Bavine must have noticed them. Although the majority of the class were migrating over to the gym, she realised who the others were waiting for. As I stuffed my textbooks into my bag, slung it over my shoulder and headed for the door she called me back. She said she had a free period and asked if I wanted her to go over the test with me. The kids at the door looked up with bored curiosity, shrugged and ambled off. There'd be other days.

In my recollection I think it was at that point that Miss Bavine developed a halo. Certainly I recall some beatific light that settled around her as she sat down at her desk, pulled out my test paper and asked me to take the chair beside her. I realised that she had just tried to protect me. I am not sure how long we sat there, going through each of my answers. It was strange realising that a teacher actually cared about me in such circumstances and was trying to help. But as I sat next to her something short-circuited in the euphoric, tangled hormones of my adolescence and I reached down and put my hand on her leg.

I know. I know. What do you say?

The world stopped in a moment.

I couldn't take it off and pretend it hadn't happened and I couldn't find my way out of the situation. But Miss Bavine just continued talking to me. She didn't miss a beat. No pause, no change in intonation. She finished going over convectional rainfall then she asked me to show her, by arranging things on her desk, how orographic rainfall works. I realised that to do this I needed two hands. Gratefully I took a book, upended it and showed a north-westerly wind approaching with a wooden pencil. Miss Bavine asked me questions about the dynamics of what I was explaining and made no comment on what had just happened. But at the end of the session she turned quietly to me and said, 'Welby, you don't have to be like the other boys. You have to believe in yourself. Hold on to what makes you different. It will be okay.'

Well, it went something like that. I can't remember exactly, but what I do remember is that I left her room and changed into my phys ed gear and instead of going to the gym I went for a run. I jogged across the rugby fields, over the road and past the compost bins and groundsman's tractor. I ran along the edge of the river that had been my solitary training ground for three years. It was quiet and I knew that the water flowed away from the school, away from the town, and away to somewhere better. Then eventually, at a corner where debris had accumulated in the last rains, I sat down on the dirt and I cried for the first time since I was a child. I thought about what she said and that she cared enough about me to tell me something so important. I realised that I loved her.

I sat there for a couple of minutes in the mud and the flotsam. Then I took a breath, pulled myself together, stood up, brushed off my shorts and got on with my life. I was going to be okay.

I have no idea where Miss Bavine is now. Like many teachers who profoundly shape us she is probably still teaching in some classroom, in some unacknowledged school, in some region far from the limelight. But she is the essence of what we must always enable and believe in. Beyond all of the ambition and posturing, the fashionable terms and career-building initiatives, she is the heart of education. She and teachers like her change lives across generations because they intuitively know how to deal with the human element in all of us. They value people.

seven things in your pocket

I know that not everybody reads books on education, but because we are here on these last pages forgive me for making a couple of assumptions about you. I think that you probably care about how you and other people learn. You think about this and at times you worry. Given the current education environment you probably do things that aren't entirely 'inside the box', but you think you should be doing more. As a consequence, sometimes you experience the professional loneliness that can be the fate of people who question.

There are probably times that you could do with a reassuring arm around your shoulder. I hope this book might offer something that approaches this.

As you will have noticed I'm not perfect. I make mistakes, so perhaps we are a little bit similar. You probably feel compromised and sense there is something better out there. I would not be so presumptuous as to tell you how to interpret what you have read in this book, but let me summarise the thinking into seven useful things for you to take away in your back pocket.

First, if you want great teachers you have to trust them. You have to give them more room to move. Don't micromanage them. They are professionals and capable of much more than they are able to exercise in environments clogged with obsessive reporting and accountability. The cultures these things build are toxic to creativity and intellectual independence. They lead to corruption, compliance and dependency.

Second, remember that the measure of performance is *not* the measure of learning. Learning is a process, not a product, and it is vulnerable. We are chronically and naively over-testing in our schools and it is distorting why and how we learn. Don't be afraid to question the value of testing. Do whatever you can to minimal- ·
ise what is comparative and increase what enables people to take risks, to fail and recover, and to think in richer, deeper ways.

Third, if you want to grow deeper, more creative people you have to build worlds where they can trade beyond experience. You have to believe in your own disobedience and be prepared to exercise it in other people. Creative thinking is normal, and learning is emotional as well as cognitive. It is fed by intimacy and passion and care. All of these things are good. Don't be afraid of them.

Fourth, you *can* change things. Don't wait for permission. You have the power. Systems are only progressed by people like you.

Change things by example. You won't get it right all the time, but most of the time you will. When you make a mistake, forgive yourself, question what has happened and build on what you learn. Don't give up. You will make things better.

Fifth, heroic leadership is a myth. It is hungry and it limits and uses people. If you put your energy into growing and empowering others you will have a much deeper and enduring influence. Your most profound changes will probably be viral. Don't render yourself incapable by throwing your energy in dramatic gestures at deeply entrenched practices. Learn how they work, then infect them with something better.

Sixth, people are essentially good and will respond to your interest in them. If they trust you, you will be able to operate in worlds without road maps where humanity, creativity and passion are a normal and rich part of learning. Such worlds will grow and attract others who will be similar to you. Look after them because you will need each other.

And finally, question bravely and constructively. Stand up for ideas. Be tenacious. Take courage. Disobey. To do this you have to believe in yourself. *Really* believe in yourself. You are your own source of power to make things better. You are the font of tenacity and wonder, the wellspring of ideas and the origin of strength. Never, never let people convince you otherwise.

a small thing in parting

So here we are standing on the last page. We will both go on with our lives and change things. Some of those things will be unaccounted and some will be noticed. That is the nature of teaching, and also the nature of influence. When we walk towards horizons that others can't see, the journey can be lonely and accompanied by doubt, but I would like in parting to share with you something that one of my students once gave me. It is pinned to my office wall. Time has yellowed the paper a little now, but the meaning is still profound. It was said by Oscar Wilde a long time ago. He was talking about people like you, about people who question and dream. He wrote: 'A dreamer is one who can only find his way by moonlight, and his punishment is that he sees the dawn before the rest of the world.'[65]

This is a wonderful thing.
Yes, this is a wonderful, wonderful thing.
Kia kaha. Be strong.

We need you.

* * *

NOTES

PART TWO: CREATIVITY

1 Cited in Fletcher, 2001.

2 Ibid., p. 31.

3 This form of problem solving is sometimes called heuristic inquiry. A number of influential thinkers have written about it, including Bruce Douglass and Clarke Moustakas (1985); Michael Polanyi (1966); Donald Schön (1983); Dave Hiles (2001); Gerhard Kleining and Harald Witt (2000); and Ivana Djuraskovic and Nancy Arthur (2010).

4 These children were initially identified as 'gifted' by their teachers and were shortlisted following a range of evaluative methods, including analyses of their early developmental histories, their volume of reading over a two-month period, their play interests, and medical examinations of 37 different anthropometric measurements. Because the children were re-evaluated at regular intervals throughout their lives, the research project became one of the longest studies ever conducted into human capacity.

5 Gowan, 1979, p. 44.

PART THREE: ASSESSMENT

6   The two essays written in 1961 were published in the *British Journal of Educational Psychology*. While both examined the effects of streaming in primary education, the first considered teachers' beliefs and the second compared streamed and unstreamed schools.

7   Although the pass percentage was gradually replaced by a C grade, this letter still related to a mark allocated somewhere between 50 and 64%. Over time, School Certificate used various groupings of percentages including the A1, A2, B1 system in the early 1970s and, after 1990, an A, B, C categorisation.

8   In the 1990s much laudable thinking on assessment *for* learning (formative assessment) and assessment *of* learning (summative assessment) entered the public domain. However, the emphasis in educational institutions has remained on the latter (assessing what is produced). Even though researchers such as Terry Crooks (2010, p. 241) have noted that formative assessment has 'more affinity to good teaching practice', what a student performs in summative assessments remains what is institutionally and nationally credited. It doesn't matter if these grades are the end point of examinations or of assessment tasks handed in as assignments during the year. We do not assess learning: we mark performance.

9   See Postman, 1993, p. 13. For a detailed history of marking in education, see Schneider & Hutt, 2014.

10   For an insightful discussion of this process, see Stray, 2005.

11   For expanded reading on the issue and its implications, see: Ayers, 1993; Kaufman, 2013; Popham, 1999; and Zhou, 2014.

12   Crooks (2010) has described its comparative role in New Zealand schools as 'low stakes'. Standardised assessment still occurs, significantly in examinations for trade qualifications in polytechnics and in the final three years of secondary education in national examinations.

13   For a graphic review of the corruption and damage to learning resulting from this process in America, see Diane Ravitch's (2010) assiduously documented *The Death and Life of the Great American School System*.

14   Despite its distinctively restrained use of standardised testing, over the past decade Finland has consistently performed among the top five nations on the OECD's Programme for International Student Assessment (PISA) – well above New Zealand. This said, assessment systems like PISA are inherently problematic and a variety of other factors need to be taken into account in an analysis of learning.

15 PISA 2012: Results in focus, OECD 2014, p. 9.

16 Ayers, 1993, p. 116.

17 Technically these children are aged between 15 years 3 months and 16 years 2 months. Normally, tests are administered to between 4500 and 10,000 students in each country. The written tests contain both multiple-choice questions and others that require longer written answers.

18 Andrews et al., 2014.

19 Indicative of this is the United States' investment in a system of high-stakes testing. Introduced by George Bush's No Child Left Behind Act in 2001 and extended through Barack Obama's Race to the Top initiative in 2009, test-based accountability is now directly linked to teachers' livelihoods. With rich rewards and severe punishments attached to students' scores, cheating (by educators and their managers) has become endemic. (See Nicols & Berliner, 2007; Ravitch, 2010; and Zhao, 2014.) Zhao suggests that fundamental to such systems is a 'disrespect of teachers as professional colleagues and intrusion into their professional autonomy' (p. 5). Children are taught a de facto national curriculum, then subjected to de facto standardised testing. Concerns with the essence and complexity of learning are replaced by performance and reporting.

20 Indicative of this are the government policy reactions in Wales. When the PISA rankings published in 2010 showed that Welsh pupils scored lower than ever before in literacy, the then education minister, Leighton Andrews, called the results 'unacceptable' and said 'everyone involved in the education sector in Wales should be alarmed'. Accordingly, in 2011 he announced a target that Wales would move into the top 20 of school systems in the 2016 PISA results table. Although he introduced a new regime of numeracy and reading testing, this did not have any impact on the next set of PISA results. In 2016 the scores showed that all areas had fallen since 2006. See: www.bbc.com/news/uk-wales-37834646

21 *PISA 2000: Overview of the Study*, p. 7: www.mpib-berlin.mpg.de/Pisa/ PISA-2000_Overview.pdf

22 These statistics were released in December 2016. See: www.oecd.org/pisa/ pisa-2015-results-in-focus.pdf

23 See www.bbc.com/news/business-26249042

24 The report also indicated that the disparity between advantaged and disadvantaged students in New Zealand was larger than in other OECD countries, suggesting that New Zealand had one of the worst equity gaps in the world. Māori students had average scores close to the average for the poorest 25 per cent of students, while Pasifika students' averages were even lower.

25 As an example, see Radio New Zealand's reporting on the 2013 results: www.radionz.co.nz/news/national/229756/nz-well-down-in-education-rankings

26 OECD Education Database 2013, Table CO3.1.A: Educational attainment expressed as average number of years of successfully completed formal education: www.oecd.org/els/family/CO3_1_Educational_attainment_by_gender_March2013.pdf

27 A graphic documentation of this in American schools is unpacked by Ravitch (2010) in her analysis of corruption in testing, *The Death and Life of the Great American School System*; in Buckley and Schneider's (2007) research into Washington's charter schools; and in Nichols and Berliner's (2007) research project *Collateral Damage: How high-stakes testing corrupts America's schools*. Accounts such as these illustrate a plethora of ethically questionable practices that can develop in educational institutions when levels of competition for funding, status, resources, students or salaries are tied to performance in tests.

28 Copies of longer submissions are normally provided in triplicate so that reviewers can take them away to a quiet corner and read them at their own pace. Sometimes we write on these photocopies, in addition to the creator's self-evaluation of the work. Where a review is to be completed at home, submissions are normally provided as Word documents or PDFs that can be annotated and returned to the originator the next day.

29 When the year is complete, students have a bound, annotated portfolio. Being cumulative, it gives parents a much clearer picture of the substance and nature of their child's progress. It is self-explanatory and infinitely more descriptive than pages of writing, or a tick-box report.

PART FOUR: PASSION

30 Significant writers include Adrienne Alton-Lee (2002); Russell Bishop, Mere Berryman and Janice Wearmouth (2014); Marilyn Cochran-Smith (1991, 1997); Colin Gibbs (2006); John Hattie (2003); Catherine Lang (2013); Parker Palmer (1998); and Ivan Snook (2003).

31 Curriculum Stocktake report to the Minister of Education, September 2002: www.educationcounts.govt.nz/__data/assets/pdf_file/0003/7491/curriculum-stocktake-mreport.pdf, p. 15.

32 Snook (2003, p. 13).

33 In 2015 Dr Scott Duncan (as a co-author) examined this issue in 'The state of play'. His research suggested that risk-embracing play is important because as children extricate themselves from difficult situations when they are young, they develop the ability to think ahead and plan strategically.

34 For example, Corkery, 2004; Burke, 2005.

35 This includes bullying, cultural ignorance and role modelling dishonest, sycophantic behaviour.

36 Ministry of Education, 2002, Executive Summary.

37 De Guzman, 2012, p. 24.

38 Jones, 2002.

39 The most recent statistics show that in New Zealand the number of male teachers in state and state-integrated schools is significantly lower than female teachers. Fewer than one in five primary school teachers are male. In 2013, 28 per cent of teachers were men, down slightly from 2012 and a drop from 30 per cent in the mid-2000s. In 2014 the percentage of male teachers at primary schools fell to 18 per cent (down 1 per cent); at secondary schools it fell to 42 per cent (down 2 per cent). Currently, in early childhood education (one of the most gender-segregated professions in New Zealand), despite a very small shift in gender balance, only 2.2 per cent of teachers are male.

40 Field, 2003; Prescott, 1990.

41 The study, published in *Cyberpsychology: Journal of Psychosocial Research on Cyberspace*, assessed the values of characters in popular television shows in each decade from 1967 to 2007, with two shows per decade evaluated.

42 Dawn Raids were a government-initiated crackdown on illegal Pacific Island overstayers between 1973 and the early 1980s. The operations involved special police squads raiding homes and workplaces throughout New Zealand, normally at dawn. Those arrested were often prosecuted and then deported back to their countries. The Dawn Raids disproportionately targeted Pacific Islanders, who comprised only one-third of the overstayers but made up 86 per cent of those arrested and prosecuted for overstaying. (The majority of overstayers in New Zealand at the time were from Australia, Great Britain and South Africa.) Although most written accounts suggest the focus on Pacific Island communites eased off after the early 1980s, immigration officers still visited schools without warning in the middle and later years of that decade.

PART FIVE: THE BUSINESS OF SUCCESS

43 Handy, 1994, p. 224.

44 Kelsey, 1999, para. 11.

45 Wasserman et al, 2005, lists these statistics in *Global Suicide Rates Among Young People Aged 15–19*, pp. 114–20.

46 See Bramhall: www.pnhp.org/news/2003/january/the_new_zealand_heal.php

47 Kelsey, 1999.

48 An EFTS is a numerical construction that stands for an Equivalent Full-Time Student. The Tertiary Education Commission determines the nature of a course by applying an 'EFTS value' to it, based on the amount of study involved.

49 Elkin, Jackson & Inkson, 2007, p. 337.

50 Peters and Roberts (1999) offer an interesting discussion of this phenomenon in their book *University Futures and the Politics of Reform in New Zealand*.

51 Curtis & Matthewman, 2005, pp. 1–2.

52 Erickson, 2012, pp. 23–25

53 This is a critical time in teaching because currently in the profession there is a high level of exodus. According to the most recent statistics, over a third of all new New Zealand teachers in state schools leave the profession within the first three years. This percentage shows a very slight decrease from Elvidge's 2002 analysis that revealed 37 per cent and Cameron, Baker and Lovett's similar findings in 2006. Although the cause can be assigned to a range of factors, including the availability of positions internationally, any organisation that loses a third of its new workforce so early in the piece has issues to consider.

54 DeWolf, 1982, p. 33.

55 What Dewey actually wrote was a little deeper and more complex. He said, 'It often seems to me that it is the deepest urge of every human being, to feel that he does count for something with other human beings and receives a recognition from them as counting for something' (*The Later Works*, v. 5. p. 239).

56 It is useful to note that both Administering for Excellence and Tomorrow's Schools were highly influenced by administration and business thinkers. The former, which became known as the Picot report after its chair, Brian Picot (the supermarket magnate), engaged significant input from non-educators such as the businessman Colin Wise, Simon Smelt from Treasury and Marijke Robinson from the State Services Commission. The

later initiative, Tomorrow's Schools, which became the blueprint for the future organisation of New Zealand's school system, was drafted by officials including Smelt and Robinson but had no educationalists at the core of its development.

57 Okri, 1997, p. 212.

58 On top of this, students generally sat exams in four or five other curriculum areas. These subjects they studied with other teachers. This was useful because they got to experience a diverse range of learning styles.

59 Across the years 1991 to 1993 the average grade in School Certificate technology in this school jumped to 62 per cent. This was well above the national mean of 48.9 per cent. Every student in the programme passed. In the five years the experiment ran in this subject, three students scored 100 per cent (all of them were girls). One class per year chose to sit bursary art/design. In 1993 there were 17 students. The average grade across the three years 1991–93 was 84 per cent. In 1992 and 1993 over half of the students in the classes (14) scored 90 per cent or above. (NZQA University Entrance, Bursaries and Scholarship results by subject, 1991/2/3, 0048). This all occurred in a school that had historically been seen as underperforming in relation to national standards.

PART SIX: INFLUENCING CHANGE

60 These theologians were outspoken critics of German National Socialism. Both Kolbe (a Polish Franciscan priest) and Bonhoeffer (a German Lutheran pastor) unrelentingly questioned Nazi policy up until their deaths in concentration camps in 1941 and 1945, respectively.

61 From his speech in the House of Commons, 28 October 1943.

62 In New Zealand, the oral examination is normally the last phase in a PhD assessment. It can run for up to two hours, and after the candidate has answered questions posed by the examiners, he or she leaves the room and a joint decision is made as to whether a doctorate will be awarded. Although there are slight differences between universities, all thesis examiners are scholars in the field of the thesis and each will have independently read, critiqued and produced a written report on the research.

63 'Proprium humani ingenii est odisse quem laeseris,' from *The Life of Gnaeus Julius Agricola*, chapter 42, section 4, p. 61.

64 Ashton Warner, 1967, p. 13.

65 Wilde, 1976, p. 1058.

BIBLIOGRAPHY

Alton-Lee, A. 2002. *Quality Teaching for Diverse Students: Best evidence synthesis*. Wellington: Ministry of Education.

Andrews, P., Atkinson, L. et. al. 2014. *OECD and Pisa Tests Are Damaging Education Worldwide – Academics*: www.theguardian.com/education/2014/may/06/oecd-pisa-tests-damaging-education-academics

Ashton-Warner, S. 1967. *Myself*. New York: Simon & Schuster.

Ayers, W. 1993. *To Teach: The journey of a teacher*. New York: Teachers College Press.

Binet, A. & Simon, T. 1916. *The Development of Intelligence in Children*. Baltimore: Williams & Wilkins.

Bishop, R., Berryman, M. & Wearmouth, J. 2014. *Te Kotahitanga: Towards effective education reform for indigenous and other minoritised students*. Wellington: New Zealand Council for Educational Research.

Blake, W. 1964. *Jerusalem*. New York: Barnes & Noble.

Bradford, D.L. & Cohen, A.R. 1998. *Power up: Transforming organizations through shared leadership*. New York: J. Wiley.

Bramhall, S. 2003. The New Zealand health care system: www.pnhp.org/news/2003/january/the_new_zealand_heal.php

Buckley, J. & Schneider, M. 2007. *Charter Schools: Hope or hype?* New Jersey: Princeton University Press.

Burke, C. 2005. Play in focus: Children researching their own spaces and places for play. *Children, Youth and Environment*, 15 (1), 27–53.

Cameron, M., Baker, R. & Lovett, S. 2006. *Teachers of Promise: Getting started in teaching: Phase one overview*. Wellington: New Zealand Council for Educational Research.

Campbell, D.T. 1979. Assessing the impact of planned social change. *Evaluation and Program Planning*, 2, 67–90.

Carnegie, D. 1936. *How to Win Friends and Influence People*. New York: Simon and Schuster.

Chou, H.T. & Edge, N. 2012. 'They are happier and having better lives than I am': The impact of using Facebook on perceptions of others' lives. *Cyberpsychology, Behavior, and Social Networking*, 15 (2), 117–21.

Cochran-Smith, M. 1991. Learning to teach against the grain. *Harvard Educational Review*, 61 (3), 279–310.

Cochran-Smith, M. 1997. Knowledge, skills, and experiences for teaching culturally diverse learners: A perspective for practicing teachers. In J.J. Irvine (ed.), *Critical Knowledge for Diverse Teachers and Learners* (pp. 27–87). Washington: American Association of Colleges for Teacher Education.

Corkery, L. 2004. Play Environments in the Sustainable Community: www.parliament.nsw.gov.au/prod/parlment/committee. nsf/0/990e4c8bc38e4eecca2571920011657a/$FILE/SUBMISSION%20 NO.27%20Assoc%20Prof%20Linda%20Corkery.PDF

Crooks, T.J. 2010. Educational assessment in New Zealand schools. *Assessment in Education: Principles, policy & practice*, 9, 237–53.

Curtis, B. & Matthewman, S. 2005. The managed university: The PBRF, its impacts and staff attitudes. *New Zealand Journal of Employment Relations*, 30, 1–17.

Daniels, J.C. 1961. The effects of streaming in the primary school: What teachers believe. *British Journal of Educational Psychology*, 31, 69–78.

Daniels, J.C. 1961. The effects of streaming in the primary school: A comparison of streamed and unstreamed schools. *British Journal of Educational Psychology*, 31, 119–27.

Davidson, C.N. 2011. *Now You See It: How the brain science of attention will transform the way we live, work, and learn*. New York: Viking.

De Guzman, J. 2012. Aspire: A creative exploration of the short, lyrical documentary. MA thesis, Auckland University of Technology: http://hdl. handle.net/10292/6359.

DeVries, T. 20 November 1945, St Lawrence Plain Dealer, Section: 'Churches and Organizations': p. 5, Canton: New York (Old Fulton).

Dewey, J. 1984. *The Later Works: 1925–1953*. Carbondale: Southern Illinois University Press.

DeWolf, R. 1982. Out to launch: Is there shelf life after Holly Hobbie? You bet. *Philadelphia Daily News*, 12 October 1982, p. 33.

Djuraskovic, I. & Arthur, N. 2010. Heuristic inquiry: A personal journey of acculturation and identity reconstruction. *The Qualitative Report*, 15 (6), 1569–93.

Douglass, B. & Moustakas, C.E. 1985. Heuristic inquiry: The internal search to know. *Journal of Human Psychology*, 25 (3), 39–55.

Duncan, S. & McPhee, J. 2015. The state of play survey: Executive report: www.persil.co.nz/wp-content/uploads/sites/10/2015/11/AUT_State_Of_Play-141015.pdf

Eicher, J. 1997. Post-heroic leadership: Managing the virtual organization. *Performance Improvement*, 36, 5–10.

Elkin, G., Jackson, B. & Inkson, K. 2007. *Organisational Behaviour in New Zealand: Theory and practice*. Auckland: Pearson Education New Zealand.

Elvidge, C. 2002. *Teacher Supply: Beginning teacher characteristics and mobility*. Wellington: New Zealand Demographic and Statistical Analysis Unit, Ministry of Education.

Erickson, T. 2012. The millennials. *RSA Journal*, 23–25.

Field, T. 2003. *Touch*. Massachusetts: MIT Press.

Fletcher, A. 2001. *The Art of Looking Sideways*. London: Phaidon.

Fowler, M. 2005. *Refloating a Stranded Curriculum*. New Zealand Ministry of Education report: http://nzcurriculum.tki.org.nz/content/download/528/3903/file/fowler_restructuring.doc

Gibbs, C. 2006. *To Be a Teacher: Journeys towards authenticity*. Auckland: New Pearson.

Gowan, B. 1979. The production of creativity through right hemisphere imagery. *The Journal of Creative Behaviour*, 13 (1), 39–51.

Guskey, T.R. & Pollio, H.R. (n.d.) Grading systems: School, higher education: http://education.stateuniversity.com/pages/2017/Grading-Systems.html

Handy, C.B. 1994. *The Empty Raincoat: Making sense of the future*. London: Hutchinson.

Hansen, S. & Jensen, J. 1972. *The Little Red School Book*. Wellington: Alister Taylor.

Hattie, J. 2003 (October). 'Teachers make a difference: What is the research evidence?' Paper presented at the Australian Council for Educational

Research Annual Conference on Building Teacher Quality, Melbourne.

Hiles, D. 2001. Heuristic inquiry and transpersonal research: www.psy.dmu. ac.uk/drhiles/HIpaper.htm

Holt, J. 1964. *How Children Fail*. New York: Pitman Press.

Huey, J. & Sookdeo, R. 1994. The new post-heroic leadership. *Fortune Magazine*: http://archive.fortune.com/magazines/fortune/fortune_ archive/1994/02/21/78995/index.htm

Illich, I. 1971. *Deschooling Society*. New York: Harper & Row.

Jones, A. 2002. Risk anxiety in the classroom: Teachers touching children: www.leeds.ac.uk/educol/documents/00002431.htm

Jones, A. 2003. Touching children: Policy, social anxiety and the 'safe' teacher. *Journal of Curriculum Theorizing*, 19 (2), 103–16.

Jones, A. 2004. Social anxiety, sex, surveillance and the 'safe' teacher. *British Journal of Sociology of Education*, 25 (1), 53–66.

Jordan, A.H., Monin, B., Dweck, C.S., Lovett, B.J., John, O.P. & Gross, J.J. 2011. Misery has more company than people think: Underestimating the prevalence of others' negative emotions. *Personality and Social Psychology Bulletin*, 37 (1), 120–35.

Kamins, M.L. & Dweck, C.S. 1999. Person versus process praise and criticism: Implications for contingent self-worth and coping. *Developmental Psychology*, 35 (3), 835–47.

Kaufman, S.B. 2013. *Ungifted: Intelligence redefined*. New York: Basic Books.

Kelsey, J. 1995. *The New Zealand Experiment: A world model for structural adjustment*. Auckland: Auckland University Press.

Kelsey, J. 1999. Life in the economic test-tube: New Zealand 'experiment' a colossal failure: www.converge.org.nz/pma/apfail.htm

Kleining, G. & Witt, H. 2000. The qualitative heuristic approach: A methodology for discovery in psychology and the social sciences: Rediscovering the method of introspection as an example: www. qualitative-research.net/index.php/fqs/article/view/1123/2495

Krasnova, H., Wenninger, H., Widjaja, T. & Buxmann, P. 2013. Envy on Facebook: A hidden threat to users' life satisfaction?: www.ara.cat/xarxes/ facebook_ARAFIL20130128_0001.pdf

Lang, C.M. 2013. Effective Pākehā teachers of Māori students. PhD thesis, University of Waikato: http://researchcommons.waikato.ac.nz/bitstream/ handle/10289/7343/thesis.pdf?sequence=3&isAllowed=y

Maslow, A. 1954. *Motivation and Personality*. New York: Harper and Row.

Ministry of Education. 2002. Curriculum stocktake report to Minister

of Education – Executive summary: www.educationcounts.govt.nz/
    publications/curriculum/5815

Ministry of Education. 2011. *Teacher Progress: What happens to new teachers in
    the years following their entry into the state workforce?* Wellington: Ministry
    of Education.

Morgan, G. 1997. *Images of Organization.* Thousand Oaks: Sage Publications.

Neill, A.S. 1960. *Summerhill: A radical approach to child rearing.* New York:
    Hart Publishing Company.

New Zealand Educational Institute – Riu Roa. 1998. *Service and Support
    Manual: Code of conduct: Physical conduct with children.* Wellington: New
    Zealand Educational Institute.

New Zealand Educational Institute – Riu Roa. 2006. *Service and Support
    Manual: Code of conduct: Physical conduct with children.* Wellington: New
    Zealand Educational Institute.

Nichols, S.L. & Berliner, D.C. 2007. *Collateral Damage: How high-stakes testing
    corrupts America's schools.* Cambridge: Harvard Education Press.

Noddings, N. 1984. *Caring: A feminine approach to ethics & moral education.*
    Berkeley: University of California Press.

O'Neill, A.M., Clark, J. & Openshaw, R. 2004. *Reshaping Culture, Knowledge
    and Learning.* Palmerston North: Dunmore Press.

OECD. 2014. Programme for International Student Assessment (PISA) 2012:
    Results in focus: www.oecd.org/pisa/keyfindings/pisa-2012-results-
    overview.pdf

Okri, B. 1997. *A Way of Being Free.* London: Phoenix House.

Palmer, P.J. 1998. *The Courage to Teach: Exploring the inner landscape of a
    teacher's life.* New York: Jossey Bass.

Peters, M.A. & Roberts, P.R. 1999. *University Futures and the Politics of Reform
    in New Zealand.* Palmerston North: Dunmore Press.

Pierson, G.W. 1983. *A Yale Book of Numbers: Historical statistics of the college
    and university, 1701–1976.* New Haven: Yale University.

Polanyi, M. 1958. *Personal Knowledge: Towards a post-critical philosophy.*
    Chicago: University of Chicago Press.

Polanyi, M. 1966. *The Tacit Dimension.* London: Routledge & Kegan Paul.

Popham, W.J. 1999. Why standardized tests don't measure educational quality.
    Educational Leadership, 56, 8–16.

Postman, N. 1993. *Technopoly: The surrender of culture to technology.* New
    York: Vantage Books.

Postman, N. & Weingartner, C. 1969. *Teaching as a Subversive Activity.* New
    York: Delacorte Press.

Power, N. 2009. To touch or not to touch: Male primary school teachers' experiences of touch: A hermeneutic, phenomenological study. PhD thesis, Auckland University of Technology: http://hdl.handle.net/10292/664

Prescott, J.W. 1990. Affectionate bonding for the prevention of violent behaviours: Neurobiological, psychological and religious/spiritual determinants. In L.J. Hertzberg, G.F. Olstrum, & J. Roberts Fields (eds), *Violent Behaviours, Assessment and Intervention* (74–81). Great Neck: PMA Publishing.

Ravitch, D. 2010. *The Death and Life of the Great American School System: How testing and choice are undermining education.* New York: Basic Books.

Richmond, R.L. 2014. A guide to psychology and its practice: www.guidetopsychology.com/famlytx2.htm

Roberts, P. 2007. Neoliberalism, performativity and research, *International Review of Education*, 53 (4), 349–65.

Robertson, J. 2007. Beyond the 'research/teaching nexus': Exploring the complexity of academic experience. *Studies in Higher Education*, 32 (5), 541–56.

Ryden, M. 2009. *The Tree Show.* Los Angeles: Porterhouse Fine Art Editions.

Sahlberg, P. 2011. *Finnish Lessons: What can the world learn from educational change in Finland.* New York: Teachers College Press.

Sahlgren, G.H. 2013. The truth about Finland's education miracle: http://blogs.spectator.co.uk/coffeehouse/2013/06/is-finland-a-choice-less-education-miracle/

Sandsester, E. & Kennair, L. 2011. Children's risky play from an evolutionary perspective: The anti-phobic effects of thrilling experiences. *Evolutionary Psychology*, 9 (2), 257–84.

Schneider, J. & Hutt, E. 2014. Making the grade: A history of the A–F marking scheme. *Journal of Curriculum Studies*, 46 (2), 201–24.

Schön, D. 1983. *The Reflective Practitioner: How professionals think in action.* London: Temple Smith.

Schön, D. 1987. *Educating the Reflective Practitioner.* San Francisco: Jossey-Bass.

Schweitzer, A. 1975. *Thoughts for Our Times.* New York: The Peter Pauper Press.

Sela-Smith, S. 2002. Heuristic research: A review and critique of Moustakas's method. *Journal of Humanistic Psychology*, 42 (3), 53–88.

Smith, E.A. 2001. The role of tacit and explicit knowledge in the workplace. *Journal of Knowledge Management*, 5 (4), 311–21.

Smith, R. & Jesson, J.G. 2005. Shaping academic identity: The politics and 'performativity' of research under government accountability frameworks:

Lessons from New Zealand. In J. Connolly, M. Leach & L. Walsh (eds), *The Politics of Recognition: Identity, respect and justice*, Melbourne: Deakin University Press.

Snook, I. 2003. *The Ethical Teacher: An introduction to the ethics of teaching*. Palmerston North: Dunmore Press.

Statistics New Zealand. 2012. Teaching staff by gender: www.educationcounts.govt.nz/statistics/schooling/teaching_staff

Stray, C. 2005. From oral to written examinations: Cambridge, Oxford and Dublin 1700–1914. In M. Feingold (ed.), *History of Universities* (Vol. 20/2, 76–130). Oxford: Oxford University Press.

Tacitus, C. 1840. *Germania, Agricola and first book of the annals*. London: Taylor & Walton.

Taylor, A. 2013. Finland used to have the best education system in the world: What happened?: www.businessinsider.com.au/why-finland-fell-in-the-pisa-rankings-2013-12

Terman, L.M. 1922. A new approach to the study of genius. *Psychological Review*, 29 (4), 310–18.

Uhls, Y.T. & Greenfield, P.M. 2011. The rise of fame: An historical content analysis: http://cyberpsychology.eu/view.php?cisloclanku=2011061601&article=1

Wasserman, D., Cheng, Q., & Jiang, G.-X. 2005. Global suicide rates among young people aged 15–19. *World Psychiatry*, 4 (2), 114–20.

Wilde, O. 1976. *The Complete Works of Oscar Wilde*. London: Book Club Associates.

Wordsworth, W. 1888. *The Complete Poetical Works*. London: Macmillan & Co.

Zhao, Y. 2014. *Who's Afraid of the Big Bad Dragon?: Why China has the best (and worst) education system in the world*. San Francisco: Jossey Bass.